Anybody's Bike Book

Anybody's Bike Book

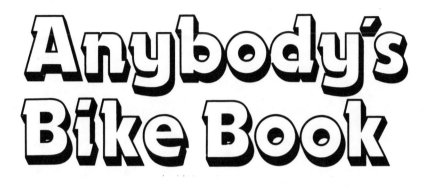

An original manual of bicycle repairs

Written by Tom Cuthbertson

Illustrated by Rick Morrall

Ten Speed Press

Thanks again, Jon Scoville

1☺

TEN SPEED PRESS
P. O. Box 7123
Berkeley, California 94707

Library of Congress Catalog Number: 84-50038
ISBN: 0-89815-130-0

Cover Design by Brenton Beck
Type set by Haru Composition, San Francisco

Printed in the United States of America

1   2   3   4   5   —   92   91   90

Acknowledgments

More than thanks to Pat.
And to Paul Schoellhamer,
Jim Langley, Johnny Thess,
Mark Michel, and Berri Michel.
Many thanks to these others who pitched in:
Dan Nall; Roger, Marcia, and Don Sands;
Phil Shipley, Syd Joselyn, Kathy Rose,
Gary Macdonald, David Morrison,
Kim Jacobs, Jim Houston,
Laurie Karl Schmidtke, Billy Menchine,
Pat and Nancy Heitkam, Michael Ray,
Mark Jansen, Bryan Loehr, Gary Barnett,
Jeff Jolin, Rick Gaytan, Brian Tailleur,
Glen (who dropped in from New Orleans
and worked at the Bike Trip for awhile),
Pete Lee, Jack Taylor, Eric Wilhelm,
and last but definitely not least,
my son, Cory Cuthbertson.

Contents

Introduction

THIS IS A BOOK ABOUT FIXING BICYCLES. It is written in such a way that anyone can use it to fix any bicycle. Many of you (especially women) may have been given the idea that if something is mechanical, you can't do it. That is outrageous. Bicycles are not monstrous machines that only wizards can understand. They are all simple enough that with a little know-how and patience, anyone can work on them. *You can do it!* You don't have to know any magic. The mechanical mystique is a lie.

A bicycle is a wonderful, practical machine, but it is fallible, like any other machine. Any bicycle needs attention. It needs lubrication and adjustment from time to time. It is subject to wear and accidental damage, both of which require repair.

Now, once there was a time when people said, if they had a machine in need of attention, "My, my, I'll have to take that damn machine down and have it attended to." They took the machine to a shop, then went off to a job where they made lots of money to pay for having their machine "attended to."

That wasn't a bad plan. It worked, and still works, for many people. But some people have started doing the whole thing differently. They now say, when their machine needs attention, "Why don't *I* attend to my good old machine, instead of paying someone else to? Instead of spending all my time working for money to pay someone else, I can spend my time learning about and maintaining my own machine."

People are starting to learn just how much they can do for themselves. They are learning to be masters over their machines, instead of slaves to them.

2

Some machines are harder to master than others. Automobiles, for instance, have a nasty habit of blowing up — a very direct and unpleasant response to a master's attention. Other machines get shorts and shoot sparks at their masters. Because of the nasty habits of these machines, people have learned to cover them up or hide them behind sheet metal and chrome. The machines are therefore hard to get at and attend to.

Consider the bicycle by comparison. No explosives. No sparks. No bothersome sheet metal and chrome to remove. Just the essential machine, sitting out in the open where its master can easily attend to its every need.

If you use this book carefully, always remembering the RULES OF THUMB, and keeping in mind your limitations and the book's (you and I are human, after all, and we are bound to make some mistakes), you can be a proud master over your bicycle.

If you go one step farther, and learn to have fun tinkering with the wonderful intricacies of your bike, who knows where your attentions to your machine will lead.

Getting a Bike

Before you buy a bicycle, think about what you are going to use it for. Then look at used bikes as well as new ones that will fit your need. A well-cared-for used bike is one of this limited planet's greatest re-cycles!

If all you want to do is ride around the neighborhood or noodle down to the store, all you need is a sturdy 1- or 3-speed bike. Even a rusty trashmo may do the trick; I have such fond memories of my old balloon-tire bomber! If rusty-trusty bikes don't appeal to you, try one of the spiffy new versions of the classic fat-tire cruisers. Put fenders and a chain-guard on your cruiser/trashmo if you live in a place where it rains. For family service, you can put a basket and a child seat on the bike and make it into a station wagon; sure, it'll be a heavy bike, but it'll work fine for errands. For kids that are too big for a child seat, there are small 1-speed bikes; if your kid is just learning to ride, make sure you get a bike that's small enough so the munchkin can sit on the seat and reach the ground with both feet. That way, you can take the pedals off the thing and let your kid walk it around to get the feel of balancing. This works much better, in most cases, than a taller bike with training wheels.

If you want to do more extensive riding in town, and maybe take an occasional jaunt on back-country trails, get a 5-, 10-, or 15-speed wide-tire mountain bike. Some people call them ATB's (all-terrain bikes). They were originally made for screaming down precipitous fire trails in Northern California, but people have found they are fun to ride just about anywhere. They combine some of the lightness and high-tech performance of racing bikes with sturdy brakes and wheels, a comfy riding position, and the cushy wide tires from the old ballooners. There are many hybrids; some have more or less gears, some have lighter or beefier components, and some are designed to be more responsive than others. But on almost all of them, you sit up more than you

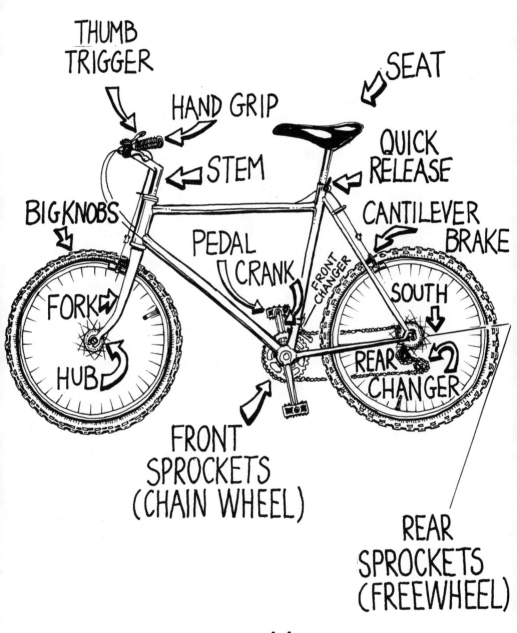

THUMB TRIGGER

HAND GRIP

SEAT

STEM

QUICK RELEASE

BIGKNOBS

CANTILEVER BRAKE

PEDAL

CRANK

FRONT CHANGER

SOUTH

FORK

REAR CHANGER

HUB

FRONT SPROCKETS (CHAIN WHEEL)

REAR SPROCKETS (FREEWHEEL)

ILLUSTRATION **1-1**
Mountain Bike

do on the racey drop-bar bikes, and you ride on wider tires.

The wide tires mean it doesn't hurt when you go over bumps, and they mean you don't get nearly so many flats when you go over sharp objects. These are both strong advantages for around-town riding, as well as for riding out in the boonies.

The sit-up position is the biggest advantage, though. It means you feel comfy and more stable than you do on a bike with turned-down handlebars. It means you are fighting a bit more wind resistance, so you can't go as fast as a comparable rider on a racing bike, but you can move right along. I enjoy the *feeling* of speed I get on a mountain bike; my head is up in the wind; my eyes are looking around me, taking in the scenery as it whooshes by. On the classic road bike, your head is bent way down in that low-wind-resistance position so you can go faster, but all you get to see is the spinning front wheel. Sure, it's spinning at the max speed, but who cares, after staring at it for an hour or two?

Speed is relative, after all. In galactic terms, we are all moving at a blinding pace toward oblivion. In more down-to-earth terms, no matter how hard we pedal *any* bicycle, we barely move in relation to passengers flying by in a jet. And yet, the jet passengers are just SITTING there, in a compartment that gives no sense of speed or motion at all. It's relatively boring. On the other hand, have you ever seen that great picture of Einstein, the mastermind of relativity, on a bicycle? He doesn't look like he's trying too hard to attain the speed of light. He looks like he's riding relatively slowly, in fact. But he's GRINNING! Mountain bikes and their city-bred cousins are a good choice if you care relatively more about having fun, and relatively less about going fast.

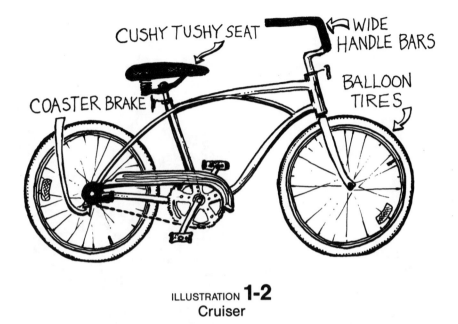

CUSHY TUSHY SEAT

WIDE HANDLE BARS

BALLOON TIRES

COASTER BRAKE

ILLUSTRATION **1-2**
Cruiser

Some of you may want to take longer country rides, though. For getting away from it all, for covering many miles in comfort and at speed, get a light (20- to 25-pound) multi-speed road bike like the one shown in Illustration 1-3. Road bikes can be fitted with carrier racks and packs to carry anything from a spare tire to full camping gear and the kitchen sink, but remember, the less you carry on a light road bike, the more you enjoy its lovely *lightness.*

For cyclists who want to take day-, week-, or even month-long trips, there are touring bikes made to cover the miles comfortably, and carry all you need to take with you. Any sturdy, light (25- to 30-pound), well-made road bike with carrier eyelets (the little holes on the frame for mounting racks and fenders) can be used for touring, but bikes with specially designed frames and extra strong wheels and tires will make life on the road easier. Mountain bikes can be used for touring, but the sit-up position gets tiresome and painful after days in the saddle.

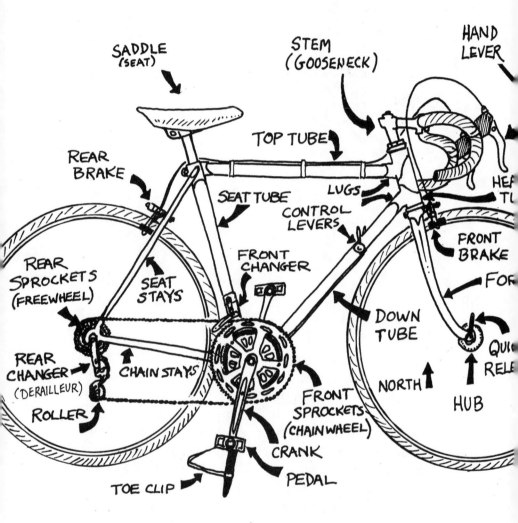

SADDLE
(SEAT)

STEM
(GOOSENECK)

HAND
LEVER

REAR
BRAKE

TOP TUBE

SEAT TUBE

LUGS

HE
TL

CONTROL
LEVERS

FRONT
CHANGER

FRONT
BRAKE

REAR
SPROCKETS
(FREEWHEEL)

SEAT
STAYS

FOR

REAR
CHANGER
(DERAILLEUR)

CHAIN STAYS

DOWN
TUBE

QUI
REL

ROLLER

FRONT
SPROCKETS
(CHAINWHEEL)

NORTH

HUB

CRANK

TOE CLIP

PEDAL

ILLUSTRATION **1-3**
Road Bike

Of course, there are those who like to race other cyclists. Ultra-light road and mountain bikes with space-age alloy components are made for racers who can afford their high costs. There are super little Moto-X racing bikes that are just as high-tech, too! For Olympic-style banked track racers there are fixed-gear bikes that weigh less than 15 pounds, and yet are strong enough to hold up under the strongest sprinters. Most of these bikes are too specialized for me to cover in this humble book.

There are other bikes than those discussed above, too. If you want to get an unusual or very elegant machine, though, remember that you may have difficulty figuring out how to fix it, and replacement parts may be hard to find. For instance, if you want to ride a recumbent (one of those long, low bikes that you ride sitting down close to the ground), try to get one that has more or less standard bike components, rather than exotic custom parts that can't be fixed or replaced.

When you have decided what type of bike you want, shop around and see as many different brands as possible. Remember, as you compare bikes, that the *frame* is the most expensive and significant part. If you buy a bike with a good frame, you can make equipment changes to suit yourself without spending a lot of money. But if you buy a bike with a heavy, weak frame, you are stuck with it. For some specific suggestions and hints, see the *Frame* chapter.

The wheels and tires are almost as important as the frame. Get wheels that are strong enough to do what you want, and as *light* as possible. Sealed bearings make sense for mountain bikers who see a lot of dust or mud. There are lots of different tires for most types of bikes. In general, you want to buy tires that grip on the surfaces you ride over, and that resist punctures, but aren't any heavier than necessary. Don't go for the super-light, custom or sew-up tires unless you race. For more info, see the *Wheels* chapter.

Take any bike you might buy on a test ride. Ride it up and down hills, around curves, over rough and smooth pavement. Ride fast, ride slow; try making quick little turns (on smooth dry pavement) to test out the steering. Be thorough. Get the feel of the bike. If it feels good, buy; if not, don't. And don't be afraid to let the color of the bike influence your decision. If you like the color of your bike, you'll ride it more and care for it better. I *love* dark blue bikes, for instance. You may like white ones; whatever you like, get.

If you can't decide between two similar brands, ask politely if you can talk to the mechanics who assembled them, and find out which bike "went together easier." The bike that works well for the build-up mechanic will work well for you, most likely. If the dealer doesn't want you to distract the mechanic, respect the dealer's judgment.

Be decent to bike dealers, and you'll find they will usually be decent to you. That sounds silly, but I have worked in and been around bike shops for years, and I've seen just how incredibly indecent customers can be. Don't expect a new bike you buy from a shop to be absolutely perfect. Bicycles are made by humans. To err is human. Use this book and it will help you overcome the human element of error. Go through the **Maintenance Checklist** with your new bike and read and follow the chapters on the parts referred to. That will familiarize you with your bike, and this book as well.

If you have trouble with a new bike, politely ask the shop people for help. Nine times out of ten, they will oblige. Especially if the shop is a good one, the kind that offers a 30-day checkup with your new bike, to take care of those new-bike problems. The fact is, some of the problems you have with your new bike might be due to *your* newness to *it.* You are as human as the people who built the bike. It takes a while for a new rider and a new bike to get acquainted. Give your relationship with your bike a little time and patience; you will be well rewarded.

Some Rules of Thumb

1. For the purposes of this book, the term "left side" means the left side of the bike when you are sitting on it, facing forward. The same is true for the term "right side."

2. On *most* bolts and nuts, *clockwise* (often abbreviated cl) *tightens; counter-clockwise* (abbreviated c-cl) *loosens.* All exceptions to this rule will be noted in the text.

3. Any two parts that screw together have threads. Threads are easy to strip. To avoid stripping threads, first make sure both parts have the same threads, then start screwing the parts together slowly and carefully. Never force two threaded parts to screw together if they resist. Some bike parts that come from different countries don't have threads that match, even though they may look the same. Make sure the threaded parts are compatible before forcing them together. And don't tighten bolts and nuts too tight. Remember — the smaller the bolt or nut, the gentler you have to be. When tightening an 8- or 9-mm nut, don't try to demonstrate your strength; show some sensitivity. Threads are delicate.

4. Think before you attack rust-frozen bolts and nuts. Is there any way you can get by without loosening that bolt or nut? Are you going to be able to replace the parts around the frozen bolt or nut if you ruin them? If not, proceed with extreme caution. Try Liquid Wrench or any other penetrating oil (you can get it at auto parts stores) before you use any tools. After you squirt some oil on, let it soak in for a few minutes, and maybe give the stuck part a few *light* taps with a hammer to encourage the oil on its way. When you use wrenches, use only ones that fit well. If you have no luck, try to find a place on the bolt where you can saw with a hacksaw without hitting the bike frame. When you have finally loosened or removed the part, promise yourself that you won't leave the bike out in the rain again. Ever.

5. Nine-tenths of the work you do to solve any mechanical problem goes to finding out just where the problem is. If you have a problem and you know generally where it is, before you start dismantling random parts of your bike, use the ***Description and Diagnoses*** sections in this book to help you get oriented and find the specific trouble.

6. Keep all bearings adjusted properly. Your bicycle has between 150 and 200 ball bearings. To keep them all rolling smoothly, you have to learn to adjust the *cups* and *cones* in which they run. Adjustment involves screwing the cone and cup together until they are snug on the ball bearings, then unscrewing the cup and cone slightly. The bearings should revolve smoothly, without any "play" or looseness between the cup and cone. Some sealed bearing sets (the cartridge type) cannot be adjusted; when they get loose, they must be replaced.

7. If you ever run across ball bearings that are retained in a round metal clip, don't throw up your hands in despair and confusion. Rejoice; you won't have to chase the bearings around the floor. Just notice, as you take the retainer out, which way it goes back in. Usually, the solid ring side of the retainer goes toward the *cone,* and the side with the gaps through which the balls stick goes toward the *cup* of a bearing set.

8. Dismantle as little as possible to do any repair. When you do have to take something apart, take it apart slowly. The more time you spend learning about the order of a unit's parts as you dismantle it, the less time you will have to spend reassembling the unit correctly. An old mechanic's trick: spread a clean rag out on your workbench, then put the little parts in rows as you take them off the unit; that'll make it easier to put them back together in the right order.

9. This book isn't about every bike in the world. Your bike may have parts that are different from the ones described and illustrated. Find, in the description of whatever

part you are working on, the *most similar* example I use. Use the description that is marked for your type of bike — road bike (rd bike), mountain bike (mt bike), or cruiser. Each section is marked for the type of bike it refers to.

10. Don't read this book without looking at your bicycle. This is a three-way conversation among you, your bike, and the book; don't leave anybody out. Step by step, do it together.

ILLUSTRATION **1-4**
How to Use This Book

11. Find a bike shop that *cares*. They will get you hard-to-find parts, give you advice, and help you when this book can't. There *are* bike shops that care. They aren't necessarily the big and flashy ones — remember, it's the people that count. When you find a good shop, do all your business there. Tell people who want new bikes to shop there. It's the least you can do in exchange for the small-parts hunting that a caring shop will do for you.

12. Cultivate a fine ear so you can hear any little complaint your bike makes, like grindy bearings, or kerchunking chain, or a slight clunking of a loose crank. You don't have to talk to your bike when you ride it — just learn to listen to it affectionately.

And speaking of being nice to your bike, here's a tip that'll save you a heap of trouble:

Always lay your bike down on the LEFT side. If you lay a multi-speed bike on its right side, you can bend, bash, and misalign its tender gear-changing parts. If a multi-speed bike FALLS on its right side, the gears are almost sure to go out of whack.

Maintenance Checklist

The three must-do jobs: There are three maintenance items that give cyclists more trouble than all others put together; check them before *EVERY* ride!

• *Chain:* Keep it oiled! The same goes for the little rollers the chain goes through on the gear changer. Keep a light film of chain lubricant (10- to 30-weight motor oil will do) on the chain, or if you're fastidious, use a spray-on dry lubricant.

• *Tires:* Keep them filled to the pressure recommended on the sidewall (see page 124 for a neato tire pressure check).

• *Hand brakes:* Keep adjusted so that the end of the lever travels about 2 inches when you apply the brakes fully. Check the shoes to make sure they aren't cockeyed or loose. [See chapter 2.]

Other things to check:

• *Bearing grease:* Any bearings that are packed with grease (wheel, headset, bottom bracket, pedal) will stay lubricated, under normal conditions, for six months or more. Any bearings that are left out in the rain or covered with sand will stay lubricated about six days. If your bearings are greased (most are), keep them out of the rain and don't oil them. Overhaul and grease them once or twice a year, then leave them alone. Use a high-grade waterproof bicycle bearing grease for maximum endurance. If you have a bike with sealed bearings and lubricating ports, get a mini grease gun from a bike shop or catalogue that caters to racers, and pump fresh grease into the lubricating ports once a year, or after any mud or dust have gotten into the works. Keep in mind, though, that most sealed bearings will stay lubricated for years, with normal use.

• *Changer:* On friction-type changers (the old kind), check the control lever adjustable bolts. If you have indexed shifting (the kind where the lever clicks) and the shifting is rough, check the adjusting barrel. Check the range of the changer and adjust with the adjustable screws. [See page 212.]

• *Creeping looseness:* Check the bolts and nuts that hold the following parts to the bike (if they show signs of looseness, see the indicated page for more diagnosis and repair): **Cranks** (page 158); **Wheels** (page 95); **Seat** (page 143); **Handlebars** (page 67); **Stem** (page 75); **Headset** (page 81); **fenders, carriers** (pages 223-24).

1
Tools

• **Very necessary.** No list of tools can be absolute. There is always another tool that might be useful in a certain situation. And there is usually some way to get a job done without the appropriate tool, human ingenuity being what it is. But this first list is really basic. These tools are as essential to bike repair as pedaling is to riding a bicycle. They're probably tools you have lying around the house. If not, you can buy them for less than 20 bucks.

Crescent wrench (adjustable end wrench). Get a good one. Attributes of a good one are: forged body, milled and hardened jaws, a precisely made adjustable jaw. To test one, open the adjustable jaw and see if you can wiggle it in such a way that it moves up and down in relation to the body of the tool. A good crescent wrench will wiggle very little, and the jaws will stay parallel. Six-inch size is best.

Screwdriver. One with a forged steel shank and a thin blade is what you want. The tip should be ¼ inch wide, and the shank 4 or 5 inches long. I used to have an old Singer sewing machine screwdriver that was given away with the machine. Its handle was just a loop of the same metal as the blade. It did almost everything and was pocket-size as well. But I lost it.

Cable clipper. The best is the heavy-duty bicycle cable clipper that grabs the cable in a diamond-shaped hole and shears it off clean. It'll cost you money but save you loads of time and patience. Get one from a dealer or order it from one of the bicycle catalogues. The chomping types of wire cutters (such as the ones on needle-nose pliers or diagonal clippers) will do, but if they are dull or weak, they mash the ends of the cables so you have to thread the cables through their housings before cutting them. If you have an indexed shifting system, you'll need bicycle cable clippers to cut the cable housing as well as the cable. Don't try to get by with diagonal clippers.

Hammer. One with a flat head is best. The smaller, the less destructive, but anything lighter than 8 ounces will be too small.

Pliers. The dime store variety is OK. To be used only as directed. Not a replacement for a good crescent wrench.

Lubricants. A light machine oil or teflon-oil mix for the chain. Also, a light-weight, high-quality bicycle bearing grease, waterproof if possible.

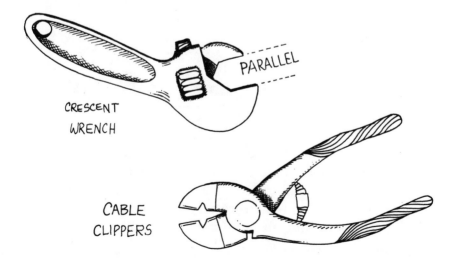

PARALLEL

CRESCENT
WRENCH

CABLE
CLIPPERS

• **Buy as needed:** The following list of tools and accessories is useful, but I don't recommend that you rush out and buy them all just to be prepared. They are described here so that when I refer to them in the text you will know what they are. I suggest you buy these as you need them or as the fancy strikes you.

Bottom bracket spanner. A flat wrench for loosening and tightening the threaded lock ring on your bottom bracket or headset. Sometimes it's hard to find one at a bike shop, or if you find one, the thing may cost a mint. Just get a shock absorber adjusting tool from a motorcycle shop that sells Japanese motorcycles. It'll be cheap and it'll work fine on most bikes.

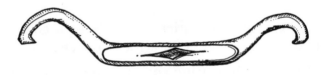

Vise-grip. Get a quality one that has jaws at least ⅝ inch wide, measured side to side.

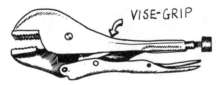

Channel lock pliers. Get a pair with jaws that can open to 2 inches or more. Please, don't get carried away with the destructive potential of either the vise-grip or the channel lock. Use them only as directed. If you want to destroy things, try squishing aluminum cans with your vise-grip or channel lock pliers. Cans recycle better than squished bikes.

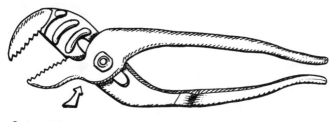

CHANNEL LOCK

Chain tool. For driving rivets in and out of bike chains. The inexpensive models work well and are available at most bike shops. Save the spare tip if you get one with yours, as they tend to come out of the tool and get lost. If you're plagued with tip-loss, you can blow some money on a fancy chain tool, or you can keep a close eye on the tip of your cheap one; when you see it flaring out like the butt end of a chisel where it's been hammered, just carefully file that flare off with a small metal file, so the tip won't get stuck inside the chain side-plates.

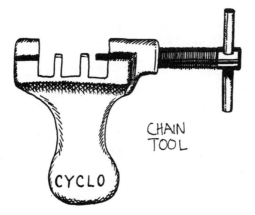

CHAIN TOOL

CYCLO

Allen or hex-setscrew wrenches. Also known as allen keys. The most commonly needed sizes are 4, 5, and 6 mm, for gear changers, brakes, and other small parts. If you have a

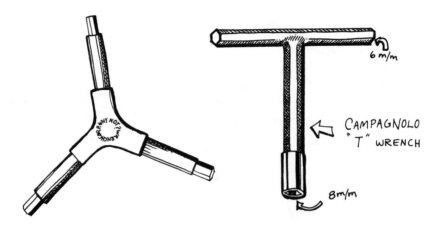

CAMPAGNOLO "T" WRENCH

6 m/m

8 m/m

very fancy racing machine, you might need 2-, 3-, 4-, 5-, 6-, and 7-mm allen wrenches. Some bike shops and catalogues sell Y wrenches with 4-, 5-, and 6-mm sizes. Very handy.

Tire patch kit. A simple little package containing all the stuff you need to fix a flat inside. The only thing you might want to add is a boot, which can be a piece of leather or a piece of thin tire sidewall, cut out to the size and shape shown.

Tire irons. Not the car type. The little ones. Plastic ones will do, in most cases. Make sure the business end of each tool has no burrs (sharp, rough spots). *Don't* try to get by with a screwdriver. Get tire irons. Get a tire patch kit, too. Bike shops have them.

Wide-jawed wrench. An old Ford Model A monkey wrench will do beautifully. A huge crescent wrench is best, but they cost a lot.

Wrench set. Box end if possible, but open end will do for most applications. Most bikes from Europe or Asia require a metric set, 8 to 19 mm. If the bike is an American cruiser, you can get an SAE $\frac{5}{16}$ to $\frac{3}{4}$ inch. Whichever set you get, don't expect it to have a wrench to fit every nut. When in doubt, use the trusty crescent.

Big screwdriver. High quality not necessary. At least a foot long.

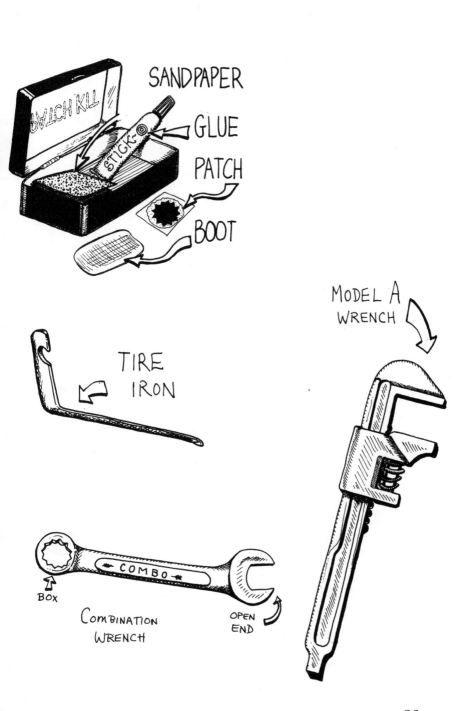

SANDPAPER

GLUE

PATCH

BOOT

STICK·

MODEL A
WRENCH

TIRE
IRON

BOX

COMBO

COMBINATION
WRENCH

OPEN
END

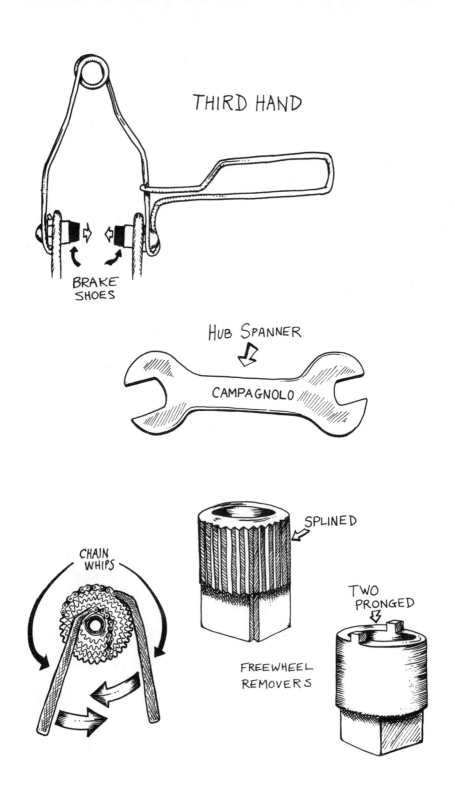

THIRD HAND

BRAKE
SHOES

HUB SPANNER

CAMPAGNOLO

CHAIN
WHIPS

SPLINED

FREEWHEEL
REMOVERS

TWO
PRONGED

Third hand. A springy, curvy little wire thing made for holding brake shoes against the wheel. Bike shops have them.

Metal file. A flat or triangular one, medium size.

Marker. A crayon will do. A red felt pen is best.

Magnet. A little one, like the ones you used to play with when you were a kid.

Campagnolo hub spanners. Buy two that fit your hubs. Either a 13- and 14-mm set, or a 15- and 16-mm set. They cost a lot, but they are essential for wheel hub overhaul. Other companies make good ones, but the cheapo brands just don't last.

Spoke wrench. A cheap item that can get you into a lot of expensive trouble. That's why they're so cheap, and available, at any bike shop that will take on a wheel you ruin. So use *only* as directed. You can get a ring-shaped spoke wrench that has many slots for different sized spokes; just make sure you use the slot that fits your spokes snugly.

Freewheel remover or chain whips. A freewheel remover is a big nut with either splines or two prongs on it, depending on what kind of freewheel it fits. A chain whip is a short length of bike chain with a handle on it. To decide which you need for your bike, look at your freewheel (the cluster of sprockets on the rear wheel of a multi-speed bike). Look at the outside end of the freewheel where it revolves around the axle. It may be hard to see in there, but look for splines, or a circular ridge sticking out with two slots in it, or a flat surface with no splines. Then see the picture of the tools and decide which remover you need: splines for the splines, two teeth for the two slots, or a chain whip for the "cassette"-type hub. Chain whip. Whew. The perfect gift for a kinky biker. When buying a remover, take your rear wheel to the shop and check to make sure you get the tool that fits EXACTLY before you use it. Don't ask me how to get a chain whip that's the right size for your biker friend, though...

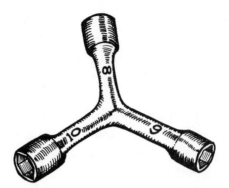

Y socket tool. A nifty little thing that fits easily in your hand, fits all those 8-, 9-, and 10-mm bolts and nuts on bikes, and gives you enough leverage to tighten them, but not strip them, if you're halfway careful. Make sure you get a well-made one; some fit too loosely to work well.

Floor stand for bike. You can buy a big fancy stand like they use in shops, but if you don't mind bending over or kneeling (I *like* doing homage to my bike that way!), you can use a simple rod-type stand that will hold the bike upright with the back wheel off the ground. You can get these stands from the better catalogues, or some super-nice shops with the home-repair guy in mind. In a pinch, you can use any car rack, wall-hook, or even a fence post to get the bike up off the ground.

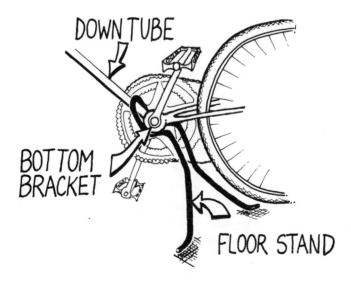

DOWN TUBE

BOTTOM BRACKET

FLOOR STAND

Two-hole vise tool. This thing will hold either a front or rear axle still while you work on the wheel. Handy, but costly.

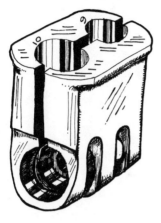

Catalogues for Tools and Parts:

Bike Nashbar
10344 Youngstown-Pittsburg Rd.
New Middletown, OH 44442
1-800-345-2453

Performance Bicycle Shop
P. O. Box 2741
Chapel Hill, NC 27514
1-800-727-2453

Cycle Goods
2735 Hennepin Ave. S.
Minneapolis, MN 55408
1-800-328-5213

For more up-to-date listings, see a new issue of *Bicycling Magazine.*

SCUFFY SKILLMAN ONE-FOOT BRAKE
(MEMORIAL ILLUSTRATION)

2
Brakes

(cl) means clockwise, and usually tightens a bolt or nut.
(c-cl) means counterclockwise, and usually loosens.

DESCRIPTION AND DIAGNOSIS: Your bike has either hand brakes or a foot (coaster) brake. The coaster brake only stops the rear wheel, and is not as efficient as good hand brakes, but it will work for children and for low-speed cruiser cycling for adults. You might have a special hand-actuated hub or disk brake, but these gizmos are too specialized for me to cover.

(Cruiser) If you have a foot or coaster brake (the kind you pedal backwards to apply, and the thing sticks, or it doesn't slow you down very well, or it slips, you have to take the rear wheel off the bike and take the hub apart to fix the brake. This takes time and patience. But the problem is usually relatively simple, so if you're short on cash and long on time and patience, follow the *overhaul* procedure on page 58 carefully, and you'll probably have the brake working fine in a day or so.

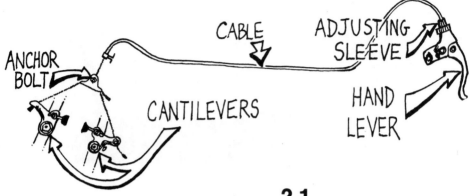

ILLUSTRATION **2-1**
The Three Units of a Brake System

(Mt bike, Rd Bike) If you have hand brakes, you can do brake repairs quite easily. The brake system consists of three units. There is a hand lever unit, a cable unit, and a brake mechanism unit for each wheel. [See Illustration 2-1.] Any of the three units can develop stickiness or malfunction. If something obvious happens, like a cable gets frayed, or the mechanism is bashed all cockeyed, go to the unit involved, below. But if your brakes get the *stickies* (a disease almost as common to brakes as the common cold is to us), *first* find out which unit is acting up. Apply the brake. Does it stay on? That's usually the rub. Heh. Move the hand lever back to its normal position. If it moves freely, it's OK and the problem is in the other two units, cable and mechanism. If the hand lever doesn't move freely, it has the stickies. [See *Hand Lever Problems.*] If the problem is in the cable or mechanism, loosen (c-cl, and you don't have to dismantle it, so just loosen) the nut on the cable anchor bolt that holds the cable at its mechanism end. Don't pull the cable out of the housing yet! Cables are hell to get back into their housings sometimes, especially if they're old and frayed. [See *Brake Cable.*] Pull the anchor bolt end of the brake cable with one hand and operate the hand lever with the other. When you release the lever, does the cable fail to return to your pulling hand? If so, and the lever is OK, then the cable must have the stickies. [See *Cable Problems.*] Cable OK? That leaves the brake mechanism. Try squeezing and releasing it with your hand, fingers reaching through the spokes and pressing the shoes into the rim of the wheel. If the shoes fail to spring away from the rim, the mechanism has got the stickies. [See *Mechanism Problems.*]

HAND LEVER UNIT

(cl) means clockwise, and usually tightens a bolt or nut.
(c-cl) means counterclockwise, and usually loosens.

DESCRIPTION: The thing you grab to put on hand brakes. The unit is attached to the bars either by one or two easy-to-get-at mounting bolts on the sides of the post, or by one hard-to-get-at mounting bolt down inside the post. [See Illustrations 2-2, 2-3, and 2-4.]

PROBLEMS: *Stickies* (Mt bike, Rd bike) If your brake stickies are in the lever unit, you have either an unlubricated axle, a bent lever, a bent lever axle, or a misshapen post. Try a

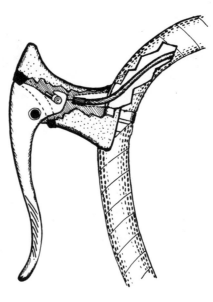

ILLUSTRATION **2-2**
Aero Brake Lever

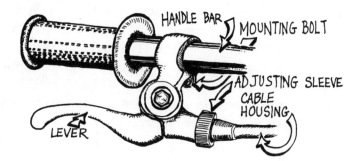

HANDLE BAR
MOUNTING BOLT
ADJUSTING SLEEVE
CABLE
HOUSING
LEVER

ILLUSTRATION **2-3**
Mountain Bike Brake Lever

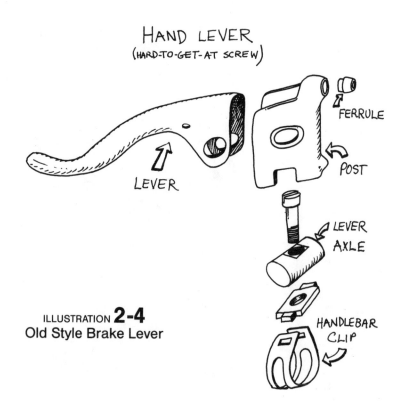

HAND LEVER
(HARD-TO-GET-AT SCREW)

LEVER

FERRULE

POST

LEVER
AXLE

HANDLEBAR
CLIP

ILLUSTRATION **2-4**
Old Style Brake Lever

little dab of light oil on the lever axle; that's the easiest thing. No luck? The most common problem is a bent lever. Is the lever out of line? If it is, try straightening it with your bare hands, holding the post in one hand and bending the lever with the other. If that doesn't help, you can try using various metal-eating tools, such as the vise-grip. If the axle on which the lever pivots is bent, you may be able to replace just the axle, if you can find a shop that has the part. If the post is misshapen, so that the casing scrapes against the lever (you can observe this symptom from the underside of the lever), try sticking your screwdriver in between the post casing and the lever and twisting the screwdriver gently to free the lever. If these procedures don't solve the problem, get a new hand lever unit. [See *Slippage* below if you have trouble getting at the screw that holds the unit to the handlebars.] Don't ever bend any brake part repeatedly without replacing it. Bending fatigues metal, and you don't want your brake to break in a moment of dire need.

Slippage (Mt bike, Rd bike) Your hand lever slips on the handlebar, or you are replacing a lever. [See Illustrations 2-2, 2-3, and 2-4.] On most mountain bike and 3-speed cruiser bars, the tightening screws are easy to get at, on a clamp around the bar. Simply tighten (cl) them.

On road bike brake levers, the screw which tightens the lever clamp on the handlebar is often down inside the lever post. To get at it, you may have to release the brake cable (that means take the tension out of the cable so that the brake lever relaxes and swings freely). Whatever kind of brake you want to release, you have to grab the brake mechanism and squeeze the brake shoes against the rim. Use the third hand tool if you have one. Stick it through the spokes of the wheel and stretch the wire loops over the brake shoe nuts. On most road bikes, there will be some kind of quick-release gizmo. It will be at or just above the brake mechanism. [See Illustration 2-9.] It is usually a little lever that you can pull toward the side of the mechanism, to partially release the brake. Take the resulting looseness in the cable back up to the hand lever and you're ready to get at the post-tightening screw. If you don't have a quick-release lever, loosen (c-cl) the cable anchor bolt that holds the end of the cable at the brake mechanism. [See Illustrations 2-9, 2-11, and 2-12.] Try to avoid pulling the end of the cable all the way out of the cable anchor bolt, especially if the end of the cable is frayed into strands. A frayed cable end is hard to get back through the little hole in the cable anchor bolt.

When you have loosened the brake cable by hook or by crook, pull the brake lever all the way down, as if you were jamming the brake on. Look down inside the hand lever post. Aha! That little allen screw head or hex nut down there is what you have been trying to get at. If you have the type with an allen screw head, you're in luck. Just wiggle an allen wrench down in there and tighten up the screw, clockwise. Counterclockwise loosens the thing, but don't loosen it until it comes out. Getting it back in is a tricky operation.

If your model has a hexbolt head down there, you need a socket to tighten that bolt. It might be an 8-mm bolt head if the bike is old or fancy. Otherwise, it is probably a 9-mm nut. Use the proper socket on a Y wrench [see page 26] or use a standard socket tool to tighten (cl) the bolt down in there. Don't try to use a tool that won't work, like your fingers, or a crescent wrench, or a vise-grip, or your teeth. You'll just mess up the nut.

When you have tightened the mounting screw or nut, you have to reset the brake by reversing whichever procedure you used to loosen the cable. A third hand is a big help. If you run into trouble, see **Cables, Brakes loose.**

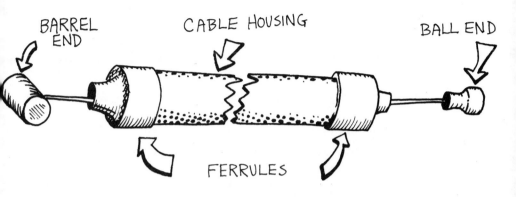

BARREL END

CABLE HOUSING

BALL END

FERRULES

ILLUSTRATION **2-5**
Brake Cable, Showing 2 Different Ends

CABLES

(cl) means clockwise, and usually tightens a bolt or nut.
(c-cl) means counterclockwise, and usually loosens.

DESCRIPTION: (Mt bike, Rd bike) The brake cable runs from a notch or hole in the hand lever, through an end ferrule which fits or screws into the brake lever post, then through a cable housing (which is sometimes interrupted so that the cable runs bare next to a frame tube), another end ferrule, and finally, through an anchor bolt which holds the cable at its mechanism end. [See Illustrations 2-5, 2-9, 2-11, and 2-12.] The housing ferrules or "sleeves" at the ends of the cable housing are often adjustable, by being screwed in (cl) and out (c-cl), thus shortening or lengthening the distance the cable goes through housing. [See Illustrations 2-6 and 2-7.]

PROBLEMS: ***Brakes loose; adjusting the brakes*** (Mt bike, Rd bike) You are screaming down the Italian Alps on your Cinelli and you see a hairpin curve coming up. Or you are noodling down to the corner market on your trusty rattle-trap and you see the grating of a gutter drain that you never noticed before, about four feet in front of your front wheel, and it looks like your wheel is going to drop between the bars. In either case, you slam on the brakes. Nothing happens for a terribly long instant. The next thing you realize is that you are watching the ground coming up at you. You should have tightened those cables, folks. It's no guarantee that you will never have an accident, but at least it will give you a fighting chance.

The idea of **adjusting the brakes** is to give the brake cable the proper tension. It's the proper tension if the end of the brake lever travels about 2 inches when you fully apply the brakes. If the lever travels much farther than that, your brakes are too loose and you may suddenly find that they don't brake. If the end of the brake lever travels much less than 2 inches, your brakes may not release completely.

To tighten a brake that's only a little loose, check to see if there is an adjusting sleeve at one end of the cable housing or the other. [See Illustrations 2-6 and 2-7.] If there is, loosen (c-cl) the lockring and screw the adjusting sleeve out *(counterclockwise)* until the cable is fairly tight. Then hand tighten the lockring (clockwise). Many mountain bikes have adjusting sleeves at the brake levers. Some don't have locknuts, because they have "clickers" that keep them from slipping.

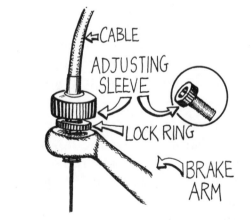

ILLUSTRATION **2-6**
Adjusting Sleeve,
Mechanism Type

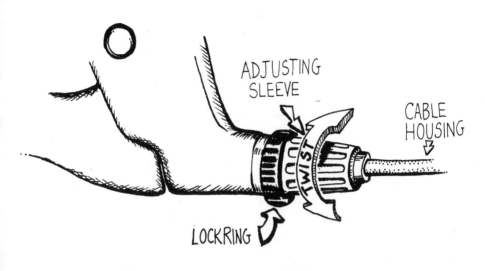

ILLUSTRATION **2-7**
Adjusting Sleeve, Hand Lever Type

Using the adjusting sleeve is sometimes easier to do if you can clamp the brake shoes against the rim while you are doing the adjusting. Use your second hand, your third hand tool, or a friend. If the adjusting sleeve comes all the way out of its threads, or even nearly all the way out, you need to take up the slack in the cable. Screw the sleeve most of the way back in (clockwise) and see the next paragraph.

To tighten a new brake cable or one that's really loose, first make sure the wheel is round and wobble-free so it won't rub against the tightened brakes. Pick up the bike and spin the wheel. Does the rim stay right in the middle between the brake shoes? If so, fine, go on to the brake adjustment below. If the rim wobbles, hops, and blips as it passes between the brake shoes, you have to straighten it [see *Rim wobbles,* page 113]. If the wheel is cockeyed or loose so it is always too close to one brake shoe, loosen the axle nuts and align it, as on page 104.

When your wheel is straight, apply the third hand. Stick it through the spokes and stretch the two wire loops over the brake shoe nuts. Make sure the brake shoes are drawn in until they hit the rim. If the shoes miss or almost miss the rim (U-brake shoes should hit near the inner edge of the rim, cantilever brakes *must* hit near the outer edge), see **Brake Shoes** below. When you get the shoes drawn in firmly against the rim, loosen the cable anchor bolt and pull the end of the cable until it's tight. Make sure the cable unit is seated at all points — that means the ferrules, the cable housing in the ferrules, and the blip (barrel end or ball end [see Illustration 2-5]) on the end of the cable in the hand lever. Everything the way it's going to stay when you panic-stop? OK. Hold the anchor bolt and pull the cable as tight as you can, then tighten up (cl) the nut on the anchor bolt. [See Illustrations 2-9, 2-11, and 2-12.]

With U-brakes or cantilever brakes, it's hard to hold the anchor bolt up and the cable tight, while tightening the anchor bolt at the same time. It seems to require a fourth, fifth, and sixth hand. You can use a tool they call a "fourth hand" to hold the cable tight, but if you can't find or afford the tool, here's a way to use one of *your* hands to hold the cable down and the carrier with the anchor bolt up. Pinch the cable between your fingers and nudge the carrier up with your knuckles. Then tighten (cl) the nut on the anchor bolt just a bit with a wrench such as the Y wrench. Don't try to tighten it too much or you'll just twist the bolt around and around, thus loosening the cable. Get the nut just tight enough to hold the cable still. Now let loose of the cable and the carrier with your other hand, grab a second wrench, such as a crescent, and do a two-wrench tighten of the anchor bolt and nut. Do it very thoroughly so you can actually see that the cable is squished inside the anchor bolt. But don't strain the bolt so hard that you strip it. That bolt is pretty small, right? The torque, or twist, used to tighten it should be pretty small.

If you have a cantilever brake with a continuous-cable carrier (as shown in Illustration 2-12), adjusting it is even a little more tricky. You have to loosen the carrier anchor bolt first, then take up a bit more than half the slack on the cable. Tighten (cl) the carrier anchor bolt, then loosen (c-cl) the anchor bolt at the end of the cable and tighten up that short end section of cable until it is equal to the length of cable that runs from the carrier to the other brake arm. This centers the brake as it completes the tightening process. Boy, is it hard to get it all to come out right. If, at the end of the process, the brake is a bit loose or tight, fine-tune it with the adjusting sleeve at the brake lever.

Now that you have the brake cable back together again, test it. Still loose? Try the whole procedure again; it takes some practice to keep all those damn things together when you're trying to tighten (cl) the anchor bolt. If the brakes are so tight that the wheel won't go around, try applying the brakes hard. Usually the cable will stretch and the housing will shrink a little so that the wheel will free itself. If just one of the brake shoes is hitting and the other one is well off the rim, see **Brake Mechanism, One-shoe-drag.** When the whole cable set-up is adjusted right, you can ride in peace. You've got a safer bike.

Stickies (Mt bike, Rd bike) You have ascertained, by the diagnostic method in **Brakes: General,** that your brake cable is sticking. The problem is that the cable is binding against a ferrule or the housing somewhere. If the cable is new, try a little oil at the ends of the housing before you do anything more drastic. If the cable is old and frayed, replace it. Whenever there are cable stickies, the cable is being worn and weakened. So get a new cable, especially if yours has frayed or broken strands at any point other than the end.

To remove an old cable, loosen (c-cl) the cable anchor bolt and pull the cable out from the hand lever end. Take the old one to a bike shop and make sure you get a new one with exactly the right shape and size end piece on the hand lever end. There are barrel ends and ball ends and mushroom ends [see Illustration 2-5], and all in different sizes. So take the old cable and match it, and make sure you are getting a new cable that's long enough. If the new cable seems too long, leave it that way — don't cut it down to size. If you have to cut a spare end thingie off (many cables have a ball at one end and a barrel at the other, so you can use the cable for either kind of brake), make the cut right next to the spare end thingie and make it a clean cut. If you make a ragged cut in your new cable, it'll be harder to get through the housing, especially if you used the mashing type clippers to cut it. If you live in a wet area, or near the beach, where your cables will always get rusty and sticky, you can get fancy teflon-cased cable and housing sets; they stay slick and sticky-free longer. If you are replacing a cable on a mountain bike or a tandem, you may want to use a super-thick heavy-duty cable. It will last longer under rough conditions. But it may not fit through the anchor bolt on your brake mechanism. If that's the case, just drill the hole in the anchor bolt a wee bit larger. Large enough for the cable, but not so large it weakens the bolt.

Now the question is: do you need to get a new cable housing at the same time you get a new cable? You may or may not. Check all the ends of the cable housings. Are they kinked or bent at the ferrules? Especially at the hand lever? This is quite often the case. Almost as often, the problem is that the housing was cut improperly, so there is a burr on the end of the housing wire that cuts into the brake cable. In either case you can cut the faulty housing end off. Cut as little as possible.

To make a clean housing cut, one that doesn't have a burr digging into the brake cable, either snip it crisply with your diamond-hole cable clipper (this works best if you have braided housing) or use diagonal clippers and slowly squeeze in on the cable housing. Wiggle and twist as you squeeze, so that the blades go in between the coils of the housing wire, instead of mashing a coil flat. When the clipper has worked its way slowly into a slot between the coils, squeeze harder and twist the clipper as you cut through.

RIGHT

WRONG (BURR)

ILLUSTRATION **2-8**
Cable Housing Cuts

Check the new end of the cable housing for burrs. [See Illustration 2-8.] Is there one pointing out into the air? You can clip it off with the mashing type clippers, or file it down. If there's a burr sticking into the hole in the middle of the housing, you have to make another cut. Remember to twist as you cut. It takes a little practice. But don't use a housing with a burr that's going to dig into your cable and gradually ruin it. Ever notice how you only break a shoelace when you're in a hurry? The same logic works with brake cables. When a brake cable snaps, it's usually when you really need it.

If your old housing is really kaput, and you have to get a *new housing,* buy a big long piece of housing, with plenty of extra for mistakes, from the bike shop. When you get the old housing out, measure and cut the new pieces the same size as the old. Use the housing cutting procedure described above. If you have braided housing, snip it off cleanly. If you have coiled housing, work diagonal clippers into a slot in the coils, then use that little twisting motion as you cut the wire to avoid making burrs. [See Illustration 2-8.] When the housing is cut to the right length, slide it into place and check to see if it fits into the ferrules. Is the diameter of the

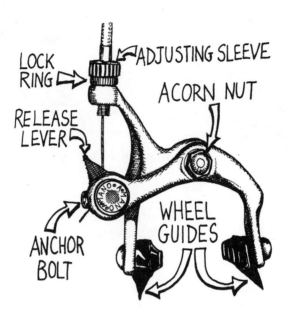

LOCK RING ⇨

RELEASE LEVER

ADJUSTING SLEEVE

ACORN NUT

ANCHOR BOLT

WHEEL GUIDES

ILLUSTRATION **2-9**
Side-Pull (Caliper) Brake

housing too big? If it is, you can strip ¼ to ½ inch of the plastic housing cover back and just stick the bare housing into the ferrule. See that the lengths of housing are just right. Put the ferrules on the ends of the housing and set the ferrules against the stops on the frame tubes.

If you have the kind of rear brake cable that has no housing along most of the top tube, make sure that the short piece of housing for the rear brake under the seat is the right size. If it's too short, it will break the cable. If it's too long, it will curve way out and hit your thigh muscle every time it bulges by, which can get to be a bug on a long, trying ride.

(Rd bike) If you have aero brake handles and cable housing that's covered with handlebar tape, make sure you can't save the housing before trying to replace it. Before you start all that untaping and taping, check for a cable joint, too; if you have one, you may be able to see a little lump under the handlebar tape, right near where the housing comes out from under it. Try pulling the housing gently there. If it slips out, thank your stars, replace only the visible section of housing, and push the new piece into the cable joint carefully, making sure it gets seated in there.

Before *threading a brake cable* through its housing, check the place where the cable end fits into the hand lever. Is it a cylinder thing with a hole in it? If so, start the cable threading procedure by running the whole cable through that hole before you thread it through the housing. If there is a little slot, thread the cable into the ferrule or handle and the housing first, then insert the cable end into the slot. To thread the new cable through new or old housing, hold the housing out straight, put a little grease or oil on the cable, and run it through, twisting it slightly as you go. Twisting clockwise? Twisting counterclockwise? Glad you asked. The idea of twisting is to keep the cable from un-raveling, right? You want to twist the cable the opposite way from the way it's wound, so that the ends don't catch and come undone. Just look at the cable and see which way it twists, and think about which way you will have to twist it into the housing in order to keep the cable from untwisting. Get the idea? Good — go ahead and do it. When the cable is all housed, check it for stickies. Hold the mechanism end of the cable in one hand and pull the hand lever with the other. Sure hope it's smooth. If not, find where the problem is, pull the cable out, and cut that section of housing over.

Don't cut the cable down to size before you have put it through the hole in the anchor bolt. Tighten up your brand new nifty brake cable according to the procedure in *Cable Problems, tighten a new brake cable.* Leave about 2 inches of cable sticking out past the anchor bolt, and clip off the extra. Ride in peace. You have a good, safe brake cable.

Brake Mechanism: General

The brake mechanism is the thing that puts friction on your wheel to stop you; when you squeeze the hand lever, the brake shoes on the mechanism should squeeze the rim of the wheel. When you release the lever, the brake mechanism should completely release the wheel. There are two distinct types of hand brakes: side-pull and center-pull. Side-pull or caliper brakes are used on road bikes for the most part. Center-pull brakes, such as cantilevers and U-brakes, are used on mountain bikes.

SIDE-PULL (CALIPER) MECHANISM

(cl) means clockwise, and usually tightens a bolt or nut.
(c-cl) means counterclockwise, and usually loosens.

DESCRIPTION: (Rd bike) The kind with the cable anchored on one side of the mechanism. The cable housing is stopped on one of the brake arms, and the cable itself is anchored on the other. [See Illustration 2-9.] The mechanism is attached to the bike frame by a pivot bolt. The pivot bolt, you will find, if you take it out, holds together a zillion indescribable parts. And the thing won't work correctly unless you get them all together exactly right. So let's get them straight. [See Illustration 2-10.] Starting at the end of the pivot bolt that is farthest from the frame, there is first an acorn locknut, then an adjusting nut, then a washer, then the longer of the two brake arms (known as the outer arm), then a washer, then the branched brake arm (the inner arm), then a third washer, then a seating pad (which is fixed on the bolt, or screwed on tightly; it has a slot in it that holds the brake spring either above or below the pivot bolt). Then the pivot bolt passes right through the frame, through another seating pad (shaped to grab the round frame tube), a lock washer of some sort, and finally a tightening nut.

What's that you say? You don't have all those parts on yours? You might have the kind of pivot bolt with a screw-head or a nylock acorn nut instead of the acorn locknut and adjusting nut. Or you might not have any seating pads. Other than that, you are missing some parts.

On the lower end of each of the brake arms is a bolted-on brake shoe. Somewhere above the brake shoe on each arm is a small pole sticking out that holds an end of the brake spring. The spring, usually a surprisingly powerful bugger, loops from one of the brake arms above or below the pivot bolt to the other brake arm.

PROBLEMS: *One-shoe drag* (Rd bike) One of the brake shoes refuses to come off the rim of your wheel when you release the brakes. First, check to see whether the whole brake mechanism is loose on its pivot bolt. If it's loose, so that the whole thing waggles back and forth, and the tightening nut [see Illustration 2-10] turns freely, just tighten that nut up (cl) while holding the mechanism by the arms so that the rim is centered between the shoes. If the tightening nut isn't

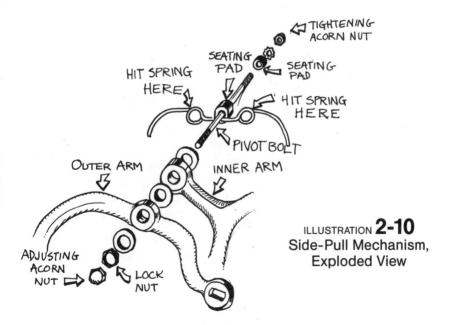

ILLUSTRATION **2-10**
Side-Pull Mechanism,
Exploded View

loose, see if there are flats on the seating pad, as shown in Illustration 2-10. Slip a cone wrench (14-mm size, in most cases) onto those flats and twist the mechanism gently until the rim is centered between the shoes. No handy flats on the seating pad? Try loosening (c-cl) the tightening acorn nut, then moving the mechanism by the arms to the right position, and tightening (cl) the nut again, making sure to hold the arms in the right position as you tighten the nut. One brake shoe still insists on coming in on the rim? Take a good look at the shape of the seating pad that is against the frame tube on the mechanism side. It might be curved so it fits the surface of the frame. If so, the brake arms are going to come back to the same incorrect position no matter how many times you loosen the tightening nut. You have to bend the spring to move the pushed-in shoe off the rim. First tighten up (cl) the tightening nut. Take your hammer, your big screwdriver, and your knowledge of these tools' destructive tendencies, and approach the brake spring from above. Set the tip of your big screwdriver on the topmost point in the curve or loop of the brake spring on the side *where the shoe is off the rim.* Got that? The opposite side from where the shoe is rubbing. Set the screwdriver as near as possible to vertical (the handlebars or the seat may make it a little awkward; the longer the screwdriver, the better) and give the screwdriver handle a tap with the hammer, lightly. No luck? Shoe still on the rim? Be firmer. But go easy. It's all too easy to bend the spring too far, or put a big nick in it, or the frame tube, or your hand. Apply and release the brakes to check your shoe position when you think it's right. If either one shoe or the other always seems to be dragging, maybe the spring is old and weak. It's time to replace the brake mechanism. See the last paragraph of *Stickies,* below.

Stickies (Rd bike) Neither brake shoe will come off the wheel when the brakes are released. You have come here

[The ultra-light
side-pull]

from **Brakes: General, Diagnosis,** or you have eliminated the
possibility of stickies in the cable and hand lever units. First,
check the nuts on the ends of the pivot bolt, especially the
acorn nut and the adjusting nut next to it on the mechanism
end of the pivot bolt. [See Illustration 2-10.] These two nuts
should be locked against each other, and *not* locked against
the brake arms. If the nuts are locked against the brake
arms so that the arms can't budge, first make sure that the
tightening nut is tightened up (cl) well. Then loosen (c-cl)
the acorn locknut, then the inner adjusting nut. The inner
nut must be tightened up (cl) against the brake arm, then
backed off (c-cl) ½ turn. Hold the adjusting nut still with a
thin wrench, if you have one, or a pair of needle-nose pliers.
When you have a good hold on the inner nut, tighten (cl)

the locking acorn nut firmly against it (not so hard that you strip the threads). The inner nut must not move while you are doing this. Still have a sticky mechanism? Try a little oil on the pivot bolt. Work the mechanism by hand, and let the thing sit a while, to get the oil worked in. Be patient. Go away, give your tires a little air, or go say hello to a friend or a spouse who thinks you spend too much of your time tinkering with your bike.

When you think the oil has sunk in, work the mechanism by hand some more. Smoother? Or still got the stickies? The trouble might be that the brake arms are rubbing together. First make sure there is a washer between the two arms. If not, that's the problem. If there is one, then probably one of the arms is bent. Check near the branched end of the inner arm (the shorter one) to see if it is rubbing the other arm. To separate binding brake arms, stick a medium-size screwdriver between them and twist firmly. They will usually spread apart easily, then spring back when the screwdriver is removed. So twist several times on the screwdriver, but go easy.

If the brake mechanism is still sticky, something very basic is wrong with it and you should probably replace it. Just remove the tightening nut, loosen (c-cl) the cable anchor bolt, remove the cable, and take the mechanism off the bike. Align the new brake so the rim is centered between the shoes, then tighten (cl) the tightening nut, and go to the *Cables* section to install and tighten the cable.

CENTER-PULL MECHANISM

(cl) means clockwise, and usually tightens a bolt or nut.
(c-cl) means counterclockwise, and usually loosens.

DESCRIPTION: (Mt bikes) The kind of brake that has the cable anchored to a carrier, which pulls on a short transverse cable, which in turn pulls the brake arms. There are two pivot bolts and two springs. The pivot bolts of the center-pull mechanism pass through a washer, the brake arm, and a hidden spring, and are mounted on pivot bosses, which are attached directly to the bike frame. [See Illustration 2-11.]

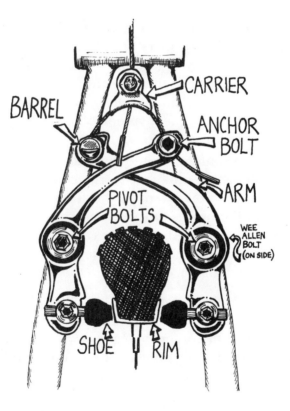

ILLUSTRATION **2-11**
Center-Pull U Brake, Bottom View

Some center-pull brakes form a "U" shape, with the arms crossing over the wheel. The bosses for these brakes are mounted on the forks or stays of the frame at a point that is *farther* from the center of the wheel than the rim.

Other center-pull brakes have arms that are moved when you pull a cam plate on the end of the brake cable. These brakes are tricky to adjust. You can adjust the cable so the little rollers travel from almost in the neck of the cam to almost over the peaks of the lumps of the cam, but if you have other problems with this kind of brake, take it to a shop for expert attention.

Some center-pull brake mechanisms have arms that do not cross over the wheel, but rather stick straight out to the sides, like cantilever rafters on a porch. These are called cantilever brakes. They have pivot bosses that are *closer* to the center of the wheel than the rim. Good, well-mounted cantilever brakes are simple, strong, and light. Alas, their jutting design makes them vulnerable to damage from the sides. [See Illustration 2-12.]

One other quirk of cantilever brakes: If the front brake cable breaks or slips out of the carrier completely, the transverse cable can flop down on the front tire, snag in the treads, slam the brakes on, and send you for a header. So keep a close eye on the front brake cable. Any fraying shows up, REPLACE it. Some mountain bikers even tie a little safety wire from the transverse cable up to the handlebars.

PROBLEMS: *One-shoe drag* (Mt bike) When the brake is released, one of the brake shoes does not come off the rim of the wheel, and the other shoe goes way off the rim. If you have cantilever brakes, all you have to do is pull the dragging shoe away from the rim and shove the carrier the opposite direction, and the brake will self-balance. If a U-brake gets the one-shoe drag, you have to adjust the relative spring tension. Find the wee adjuster allen bolt that goes into one of the arms of the brake from the side, near the

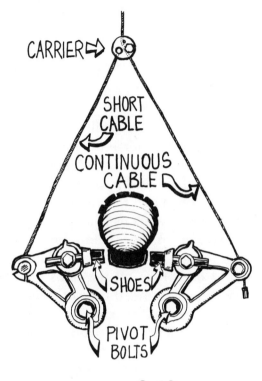

CARRIER ➪

SHORT
CABLE

CONTINUOUS
CABLE ➘

SHOES

PIVOT
BOLTS

ILLUSTRATION **2-12**
Cantilever Brake

pivot. [See Illustration 2-11.] Find the tiny allen wrench that fits in there (often a 2-mm one) and turn the adjuster bolt in and out until the rim is centered between the brake shoes.

Stickies (Mt bike) The brake shoes do not release the rim of the wheel when you release the hand lever, and you have checked the cable and lever for stickies. The problem is either unlubricated pivot bolts, bent brake arms rubbing together, or a broken brake spring.

Try a little oil on the pivot bolts. To work the oil in, first *release the brakes.* On some models this can be done by squeezing the shoes onto the rim by hand, or with the third hand, and then just slipping the barrel on one end of the short transverse cable out of its curved prongs.

When the short transverse cable is released, try working

the brake arms in and out by hand. Still sticky? You oiled in vain? On U-brakes, check to see if the arms are bent and jamming against each other. On most models, the arms should not touch each other at all; the two surfaces should be flat and clear of each other. If they aren't, pry them gently with a screwdriver. If it takes a lot of prying to get the arms free of each other, they must have been given quite a bash to get so bent out of shape. Consider getting a new mechanism. Bending metal weakens it, and rebending it to get it straight weakens it again. Don't tempt brake breakage.

If you're going to get a new mechanism, you'll have to take off the old one. Take off the transverse cable as described above, then remove the pivot bolts that hold the brake arms. Take your old mechanism to a bike shop and get an exact replacement. When you put on a new mechanism, make sure you set the springs in the same holes on the bosses, if there are several spring holes there. Set the brake shoes straight and tighten up (cl) the nuts that hold them. [See *Brake Shoes.*] On U-brakes, you must next loosen (c-cl) the locknuts on the pivot bolts, pull the shoes away from the rim (so the other ends of the arms are all the way down, then tighten (cl) the locknuts on the pivots, so the springs will have equal tension. To set the cable on your nice new mechanism, see *Cables, tighten a new cable.*

Broken transverse cable (Mt bike) If the short cable that crosses from one brake arm to the other is broken or frayed, you've got to replace it. There are two different types (as with almost everything else about brake mechanisms). One type is a single simple cable with a barrel on one end and an anchor bolt at the other end. [See Illustration 2-11.] The other type has a continuous cable that passes right through an anchor bolt in the carrier and runs out to a second anchor bolt on one of the brake arms; an additional short cable with barrels at both ends connects the carrier to the other brake arm. [See Illustration 2-12.]

With the single simple type, *replacement* is simple. Apply the third hand to the brake shoes. Stick the barrel in the fork at the end of one of the brake arms, then thread the cable through the carrier. Then thread the loose end through the anchor bolt at the end of the other brake arm. Tighten the cable as much as possible, then tighten (cl) the cable anchor bolt thoroughly, until the cable is visibly squished. If you need to tighten up the main cable a bit, you can do it with the adjusting sleeve at the brake handle, or adjust the main cable.

To replace the short transverse cable that connects the carrier to one brake arm on the continuous cable type set-up as shown in Illustration 2-12, first slip the barrel end out of the fork in the end of the cantilever arm. Then loosen (c-cl) the anchor bolt in the carrier. To hold the carrier still while you turn the nut, stick an allen wrench in the little hex hole next to that nut. Loosen the nut most of the way off its bolt, then spread apart the two pieces of the carrier and slip the barrel at the end of the short transverse cable out of its nook. Make sure the new cable is the same length as the old one, and put the single barrel at one end into the carrier nook the old one came out of. Did the continuous cable come out of the carrier? That's to be expected. Slide the carrier around the cable, push the two pieces of the carrier together so the barrel is in its nook and the continuous cable is in place, then tighten (cl) the anchor bolt nut with your fingers, just enough so the whole thingie will stay together. Then find the place on the continuous cable where the anchor bolt was pinching, and place the carrier there. Put an allen wrench in the little hex hole next to the anchor bolt's nut, and tighten (cl) the nut firmly. Then push the barrel at the other end of the short cable into its fork at the end of the brake arm, (if there are two barrels on the cable, use the one that's not at the end. Try the brake out. You may have to adjust the main brake cable, so turn back to **Tightening a new cable,** page 37.

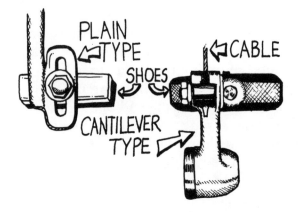

ILLUSTRATION **2-13**
Brake Shoes, Two Types

BRAKE SHOES

(cl) means clockwise, and usually tightens a bolt or nut.
(c-cl) means counterclockwise, and usually loosens.

DESCRIPTION AND DIAGNOSIS: (all bikes) There are two types of brake shoes. The most common type is mounted by a bolt to the brake arm. This type appears on all side-pull brakes and some center-pull brakes (that's the *plain type* in Illustration 2-13). On most cantilever brakes, the shoe is attached to a smooth pole, which is in turn clamped tight to the brake arm by an eyebolt (the cantilever type in Illustration 2-13). All this means is that the cantilever type can pivot as well as slide up and down. This makes it a little harder to be sure that the brake shoe stays straight as you tighten up on the nut that holds it, but there's a good reason for the complication. The eyebolt allows you to change the angle at which the brake shoe hits the rim. Some rim walls flare out more than others. You can set the eyebolt brake so that it not only hits the rim, but hits it flush, no matter how much your rim wall flares out. This will give you excellent braking power.

PROBLEMS: **_Brake shoes cockeyed_** (all bikes) The brake shoes are not grabbing the rim correctly, because they are too high or too low, or because they are not parallel to the rim. Brake shoes are pretty simple. They are held to the brake arms by a bolt and a nut (or an eyebolt and a nut). Loosen (c-cl) the nut, and you can set the shoe by hand so that it will hit the rim correctly. Make sure that the shoe is both parallel to the rim and at the right level so that it grabs the rim when you apply the brakes and not the tire above or nothing below. If the brake shoe goes into the tire, it tends to wear the tire out. Fast. ZZZZZ BAM! Like that. When you get the shoe where it should be, hold it there while you tighten up (cl) the nut. Careful. Those bolts strip easily. Now check it to make sure the shoe didn't move while you were tightening. If you have the type of brake shoe with an eyebolt, as on many mountain bikes, make sure you haven't tilted or slid the shoe to some new position. When you put on the brakes, both shoes should squeeze toward each other at the same angle.

    Brake shoe toe-in (all bikes) Your brake shoe might be cockeyed, not up and down, but in and out, so that one end of the shoe toes in and hits the rim way before the other. Don't worry if the front end of the shoe hits a little before the rear end; some people even prefer their shoes toed in that way. Do worry though if the rear end of the brake shoe is hitting first. The problem is that the brake arm or a shoe is bent. Replace a bent shoe. To straighten a bent arm, use a crescent wrench with care. Apply it to the arm either just above or below the brake shoe (don't grab the brake shoe assembly with that wrench — it will destroy that thing before you can blink). Turn it gently until the shoe is at the proper angle. It doesn't take much to get it right. And it doesn't take much more to twist the thing right off. If that happens you'll have to get a whole new mechanism, as replacement arms are very difficult to come by.

(Mt bike) On many mountain bikes you can adjust the brake shoe toe-in precisely because the eyebolt can be pivoted fore and aft as well as up and down. Loosen (c-cl) the nut and gently wiggle or shift the shoe to get it set so the front edge hits barely before the back edge. Make sure you keep all the other aspects of the shoe alignment the same, though. This can be tricky. You may want to have a pro brake adjuster at a shop do the job once, then you just do minor adjustments in the future, keeping the alignment that was originally set by the pro.

Worn brake shoes (all bikes) Your brake shoes are worn down to the metal, or hardened with old age. *Warning:* If your brakes make you feel insecure, don't just replace the brake shoes and go on your way, hoping for the best. If something about the brakes is spooky, chances are that changing the shoes won't solve much. Check the rest of the brake system. The actual process of changing the brake shoes is simple. If you have a mountain bike with eyebolt-mounted brake shoes that can pivot all over the place, you may want to replace one shoe at a time, matching the alignment of the remaining shoe with the first new one, then matching that with your second replacement.

To replace a shoe, unscrew (c-cl) the nut that holds the brake shoe, remove the shoe, and take it with you to get replacements. Replace the whole shoe, bolt and all. You have to get the same type (plain or eyebolt) [see Illustration 2-13] that your old ones were, because the new ones will have to fit the old arms. If you have trouble getting adequate braking power, especially in hot or wet weather, you can get special brake shoes with cooling fins, super-duper abrasive rubber, and optimum shape. Wow. In wet weather, you can make normal brakes work OK if you apply the brakes lightly *before* you need to stop; this whisks off the water so the brake can grip. Notice how the rubber on your old shoes is worn at a certain angle. If you have the plain type brake shoes, you should try to find replacements that have rubber pads with a similar angle. Or if you have the eyebolt type brake shoes, you adjust the brake shoes to fit the rim as you install them. If your new shoes only have metal stops at one end, make sure you put them on with the metal stops in front of the rubber pads (that is, toward the front of the bike).

Brake shoes squeaking (all bikes) When you apply the brakes, your whole bike vibrates, and, if you are going fast, your brakes screech like a Model T Ford with its original brake shoes. My own brakes often sound like this, and I don't let it bother me too much, as long as the brakes still do their job. But if the sound bothers you, first check the rims of the wheels. Are there streaks on the rims where some of your brake shoe rubber has worn off onto the metal and stuck there? That might be it. Clean the rims with Ajax or some other cleanser (nothing so strong that it will damage the smooth surface of the rim, like steel wool) and look for uneven places on the rims. It doesn't take much to make a brake shoe start rubbing off on a rim. You might need a new rim. See *Spokes and Rims,* page 111. The next thing is to adjust the toe-in. [See *Brake shoe toe-in.*] It may stop your squeaking to bend the brake arms slightly with a crescent wrench (easy — remember, they break easily) so that the front ends of the shoes hit a little before the rear ends. But don't get carried away. The whole length of the shoe should hit the rim if the brakes are put on hard. If your brakes still screech, don't fret, as long as they work.

If the brakes "judder" so the whole bike shakes, this may be due to a loose long bolt or pivot bolt (the bolt that holds the mechanism to the frame). Tighten (cl) the bolt and see if the mechanism still chatters away against the frame when you apply the brakes. If it does, it may be bent, or you may just have to put a bigger washer and/or seating pad between the mechanism and the bike frame [see Illustrations 2-10, 2-11, and 2-12].

Coaster Brakes

(cl) means clockwise, and usually tightens a bolt or nut.
(c-cl) means counterclockwise, and usually loosens.

(Cruiser) *To Overhaul a Coaster Brake Hub,* first take the rear wheel off the bike. See page 96 if you need help doing this job. If taking the wheel off seemed like a huge hassle to you, consider taking your brake problem to a good bike shop. If taking the wheel off was easy and got you all curious about what kind of a spiffy mechanical puzzle you were going to find inside the hub, then you'll probably do fine on this overhaul yourself.

Before you start wildly unscrewing all the things that keep the guts of the hub inside there, though, pause a sec, clean up your work area, clean the hub off, and figure out a way to hold the wheel still while you're working on it. A brake hub has quite a few little parts in it, and if they get dirty or out of order before you put them all back together, the hub will not work right later.

So, start by cleaning all dirt and gunk off the outside of the hub. If you've been out riding in the swamps or cruising the sand dunes, it may even make sense to take the wheel to a do-it-yourself car wash and blast the gunk off with a hot water jet. Then take a stiff wire brush and clean out the threads of the axle ends as well as you can. This will make all the threading on and threading off of small hub parts easier during the overhaul.

Next, lock the brake arm tightly in place on its end of the axle. This is done by holding the arm still with one hand and getting a wrench that fits snug on the locknut, then tightening (cl) that locknut hard against the brake arm. If the locknut is just a thin one, like in Illustration 2-14, unscrew (c-cl) the axle nut, get about four thick washers that will fit around the axle, then tighten (cl) the axle nut back down, so it can help hold that brake arm tightly in place.

Now hold the wheel flat, so the brake arm end of the axle is sticking straight down, and clamp the nut that is at the lower end of the axle in a vise. You got no vises? Good for you. A C-clamp will do the trick. Just hold the wheel flat at the corner of a table, so the brake arm end of the axle is sticking straight down past the corner, and the brake arm itself is resting *on* the corner of the table. Then clamp the brake arm firmly with a C-clamp. If you not only have a vise, but a slick two-hole axle vise tool, you can just stick the end of the axle into the big hole of the vise tool and tighten the vise up on it.

OK, one way or the other you have your wheel held in place horizontally, with the end of the axle that *doesn't* have the brake arm sticking *up*. Take the axle nut off (c-cl) that upper end of the axle, holding onto the wheel and brake arm with your free hand to keep things still. The axle should not spin, even if the threads on it are a bit rough. If the axle does spin when you turn the nut, you haven't locked the nuts on the other end tight enough. Go back and do that over.

Put the nut down on a clean rag on your bench, at one end of the rag, so you can line all the other brake parts up next to it as you take them off. If there is a serrated washer under the nut you just took off, take off the washer and place it next to the nut, with the bumps down, just like they were when the washer was around the axle. That way, when you go to put the washer back on the axle, you won't have to wonder which way is right side up.

Next look closely at the sprocket and the shiny dust cap that is just under it. Do they look OK? No bent or chipped teeth on the sprocket, no cracks or bent-out places on the dust cap? Ring spring tight in its groove? If those things are all OK, and your chain hasn't been skipping due to the sprocket being extremely old and worn down, then skip the next two paragraphs and get on with the brake overhaul.

If your sprocket or dust cap are shot, you have to take the sprocket off. Get a skinny-ended screwdriver and stick it between the ring spring and the fat driver it is stretched around; there are little crescent-shaped gaps cut into the side of the driver where your skinny screwdriver tip will fit easily. Pry one end of the ring spring out from the driver, then move on to the next gap, so the spring will work its way out of the groove from one end to the other. Hold your free hand above the spring, like a shield wrapped around the end of the axle, so the spring can't leap up and poke your eye out, or fly across the garage and roll down the driveway headed for the land of never-never.

When the spring is off, take off the sprocket and the dust cap, and place them on your clean rag, with the same side facing up that was facing up on the wheel. Get the replacement parts you need, making sure they are exactly the same as the originals, and put the dust cap, sprocket, and ring spring back around the driver just the way they were before. Make sure the sprocket is "dished" the same way it was before. Wonder how you get that ring spring stretched on there? Just start one end in the groove, then work your way around the spring from that end, holding the other end of the spring down, and prying with the skinny screwdriver at each little crescent-shaped gap so the spring stretches out and around that fat driver.

To proceed with the brake overhaul, loosen (c-cl) the locknut that's the next thing in line on the axle. Take it off, put it in line on your clean rag. Loosen (c-cl) the threaded cone that's next on the axle, and put it next in line on the rag.

Next lift out the retainer of ball bearings. (If there is a thin dust cap holding them in, pry that out very carefully with a screwdriver, working around and around the ring as you pry, to keep the little thing from getting bent.) When you get the retainer full of its ball bearings out of the hub, put it right down on the clean rag, with the same side of the

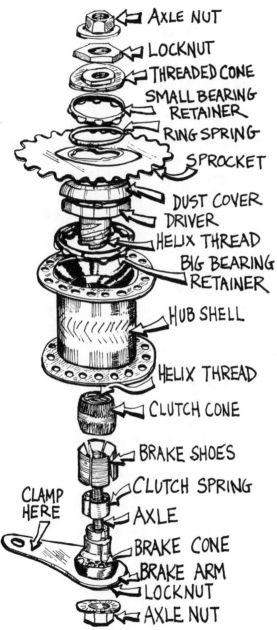

AXLE NUT

LOCKNUT

THREADED CONE

SMALL BEARING RETAINER

RING SPRING

SPROCKET

DUST COVER

DRIVER

HELIX THREAD

BIG BEARING RETAINER

HUB SHELL

HELIX THREAD

CLUTCH CONE

BRAKE SHOES

CLUTCH SPRING

CLAMP HERE

AXLE

BRAKE CONE

BRAKE ARM

LOCKNUT

AXLE NUT

ILLUSTRATION **2-14**
Coaster
Brake Hub

ring up that was up when the retainer was in place. Say, you're making a pretty professional-looking row of parts on your clean rag! Keep things straight like that, and you'll get a rewarding feeling when you put the wheel all back together and it works perfectly, with no parts left over.

The next thing to take out of the hub is the driver and sprocket assembly. Hold the wheel hub down against the brake arm end of the axle and turn the sprocket slowly (c-cl); it will spin right up out of the hub on its large helix threads. Set the whole assembly down on the clean rag, lift the large bearing retainer ring out of the hub shell, and put it down by the driver assembly.

Still holding the wheel in place? Good. Now lift it with one hand, slowly, and catch any loose brake parts that slip out around the brake arm as the rising hub shell clears them. On the type of hub illustrated, two or three brake shoes may come slipping down out of the hub. On other brakes, four little shoes might come tumbling out, or you may find that there is a whole stack of thin brake discs around the axle. That's OK, just catch any brake shoes that do fall, and put them in a line on the clean rag.

Set the wheel aside, then slide the clutch cone up off the axle and put it in order on the clean rag. On different brakes there are clutch cones of all sizes and shapes, but they all have the big helix threads inside them, and they all pull the clutch tight when you pedal forward, and push over against the brake shoes or discs when you backpedal. You may want to put the driver and the clutch cone together right now, threading helix to helix (cl), so you can figure out for yourself how the whole hub works. Get the idea? Isn't it lovely?

After you've put the driver and clutch cone down on the clean rag, the only things left on the axle that you can take off are the clutch spring, and maybe (on some brake types) a pile of brake discs or a single brake spring washer.

Clean all of the parts, one at a time, including the bearings still on the brake cone, and the inside of the hub shell. Replace the clutch spring, no matter what problem you had with your brakes. If your hub has both a clutch spring and a brake shoe spring, replace both of them.

Then check the helix threads of the driver and clutch cone to make sure they aren't chipped or worn away. Check the brake shoes to make sure they aren't either worn smooth on the outer surfaces, or bent, or marred by a little burr somewhere on the braking surface. If you have brake discs, see that they aren't burred or glazed over with old dry grease. Check the inside of the brake hub to make sure it isn't all scored or marred by burrs. All those brake surfaces have to be perfect for the brakes to work right.

Take a steel ruler and line its edge up with the axle to make sure the axle isn't bent. Look closely at the bearing dust caps and make sure none of them are bent. Check the bearings to make sure they aren't pitted or worn flat.

Replace any parts that are wrecked. You may want to draw a little picture of any part you have to take to a shop; leave the picture of the part right in the place where the part went on your clean rag lineup, so you won't forget how to set the thing back in place for quick reassembly.

OK, got all the new parts you need? Bet it was a pain finding them, wasn't it? And a shock to learn how much they charge for some of those simple little things. Such is life.

Clean all the parts again, new and old, including the brake arm and cone assembly that are still attached to the axle. Use a safe but strong solvent for gunk removal, and after each part is clean, make sure it *stays* clean until it is safely back inside the hub. A bit of grit in the wrong place inside a brake hub can totally ruin the thing. If the hub gets ruined, you'll have to go through this whole process AGAIN. You wouldn't want to do that, now, would you? So get anal.

Start the **Brake Hub Reassembly** by spreading a bunch of good multi-use grease on the bearings that are on the brake cone you left locked in place on the axle. (Beware; some types of bike grease will glaze over at the high temperatures that build up inside a brake hub.) Then put your NEW clutch spring and/or brake shoe spring in place. If you have a washer for either spring, put it on first.

Next you have to grease the brake shoes (or discs), hold them in place around the brake cone, slide the clutch cone down the axle until it nestles against the brake shoes, and finally slide the wheel over the whole business. This can be tricky. Use lotsa grease on the brake shoes, and they may stay in place while you slide the wheel down over them.

You may even have to take the axle out of whatever device is holding it, turn the axle horizontal, then hold the brake shoes in place and slide the hub over them. However you do the trick, make sure the shoes wind up snug against the fixed brake cone, and lined up with the "key" bumps and the slanting faces of both the brake and clutch cones, so the brake shoes stay in place when the wheel is whirling around them. When you get the hub resting down flush on its bearings, hold it against them and turn it, peering down into the hub at the brake shoes as you do so. Brake shoes snug down against that fixed brake cone? Wheel sliding around them without any hang-ups? Good.

The wheel will wobble and wiggle as you turn it on just that single set of bearings, of course, but the brake shoes shouldn't flop around down in there, or get jammed catty-whompus against the turning hub shell.

When you're sure you have the brake parts lined up right inside the wheel, put the big retainer of bearings into its race in the hub shell, grease the bearings, and turn (cl) the driver assembly down into the clutch cone on its helix threads, until it rests against the bearings.

Next put the small retainer of bearings into the race on top of the driver assembly, grease them, and spin (cl) the cone down the axle until it is snug against the bearings. Back it off a bit (c-cl), hold it with one hand, and use the other hand to turn the sprocket (cl) as it would turn if you were pedaling the bike. Turn the sprocket, hold it still and let the wheel coast, then turn the sprocket the other way (c-cl), as if you were backpedaling.

Do you feel a nice smooth application of the brakes? Does the wheel slow quickly and quietly to a stop? If not, take the cone, bearings, and driver assembly off the axle, and take the wheel off if you have to in order to get those brake shoes and their cones in line so they coast and brake like they're supposed to.

If you can't get it together so it works when you put all the stuff on the upper end of the axle, take the wheel to a pro and ask him or her if you can watch the thing being put together so it will work. That way you'll learn the tricks, and you won't be afraid to take the thing on again if you have to later.

When the brake is working smoothly, tighten (cl) the threaded cone again by hand, then back it off about ¼ turn, or until you can just *barely* feel some play if you wiggle the rim of the wheel gently with your fingertips. Turn (cl) the locknut onto the axle and tighten (cl) it against the threaded cone. Try to get hold of a cone wrench that's big enough to fit the cone and hold it still while you tighten the locknut, so you can be sure the hub will keep the precise adjustment you have just given it. If the hub gets too tight, you can ruin the bearings. If it's too loose, the axle may bend or the driver may fatigue and snap. So get it right.

Take the wheel out of the vise or whatever was holding it, then put the washers (if you have any) on both ends of the axles (serrated bumps facing IN, remember), and thread the axle nuts on (cl).

Put the wheel on the bike, turning to page 100 if you need any hints. Then air up the tire and ride in peace. You've got good brakes again!

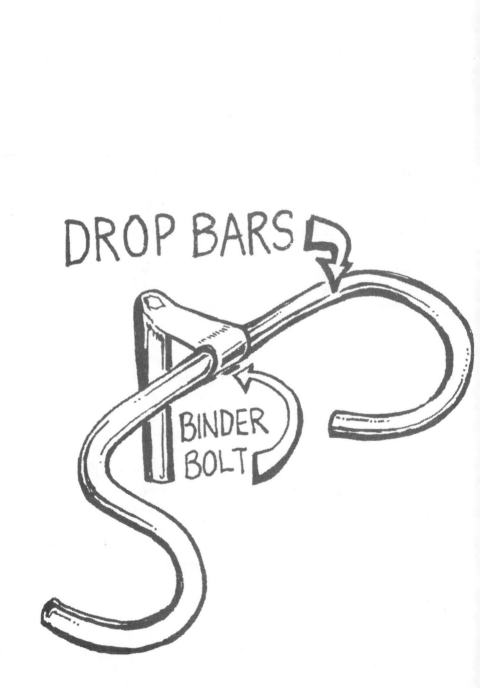

DROP BARS

BINDER BOLT

3
Handlebars

(cl) means clockwise, and usually tightens a bolt or nut.
(c-cl) means counterclockwise, and usually loosens.

DESCRIPTION: (all bikes) Handlebars, made of steel or aluminum, come in many different shapes. The curved-down drop bars are most common on road bikes; mountain bikes often have almost straight bars. [See Illustration 3-1.] Mountain bike bars are often held in a custom chrome-moly steel tube stem. If you have drop bars (Maes, or turned-down), you can add a clip-on aerodynamic bar, like the one Greg LeMond used when he won the time trial at the end of the 1989 Tour de France. Just keep in mind that no matter what anybody says, HE won that race, the bars did not. Riding in that hands-far-forward position will not automatically increase your speed by 10 percent. It may make you more aerodynamic, but it may also make you very unstable, especially if you have to turn or stop suddenly. For anything but time trials and triathlons, I think drop bars, mountain bike bars, or the simple aero bars that have no dip (like the ones made for mountain bikes) make the most sense. Drop bars can be set in a wide variety of positions. The faddish, upside-down position is unsafe. It invites impalement. You like it? You can have it. Speaking of impalement, handlebars must *always* have something over or in their open ends. I

67

ALLROUNDER

CLIP-ON BAR

DROP BARS
BINDER BOLT

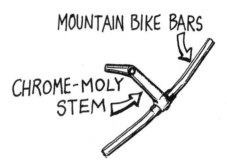
MOUNTAIN BIKE BARS
CHROME-MOLY STEM

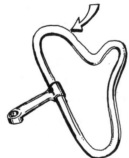
TRIATHLON BARS

BA-BARS

ILLUSTRATION **3-1**
Handlebars

don't care if it's a super-adjustable neoprene plug, or a molded custom-fit grip, or an old champagne cork; just keep something stuck in the ends of your handlebars. I literally owe my life to the fact that I've always had my bars plugged.

The handlebars are held to the stem by either a fixed binderbolt and a nut, or a binderbolt that tightens into a threaded hole. [See Illustration 4-1.] Mountain bike and all rounder bars usually have grips, and drop bars are usually wrapped with cloth or plastic tape to improve the rider's grasp.

PROBLEMS: *Bars loose in stem* (all bikes) That means the handlebars slip around, but the stem does not. Position the bars to your taste and tighten up (cl) the binderbolt. If you have a fixed binderbolt and nut, and tightening up the nut just spins the binderbolt around, the key or "dog" that's supposed to hold the binderbolt still has been sheared off. Loosen (c-cl), the nut, holding the bolt head with a vise-grip if necessary. Take the sheared-off bolt to a shop and get an exact replacement. If the slot in the handlebar for the key has been ruined, get the kind of binderbolt that has a hex head on it so you can hold it with a wrench. Reassemble [see Illustration 4-1].

Whatever kind of binderbolt you have, make sure you get it very tight. First put a drop of oil on the threads of the bolt so you can cinch up smoothly. Check the fit of your wrench (a box end wrench is best, and a carefully used crescent is better than a loose open end wrench), then really tighten up. Test for slippage by pushing and pulling on the bars.

If your handlebars slip because they are obviously too small in diameter for your stem, you can get a shim (sometimes called a ferrule), a thin, curved strip of metal which fits between the bars and the stem, so that the stem can be bound up snug on the bars. You have to get the exact right shim, especially for a mountain bike, or the bars will come loose.

Bars too high or low (all bikes) To raise or lower the handlebars, you have to loosen (c-cl) and tap on the expander bolt (the one in the stem) so the stem can slide up and down [see Illustration 4-1]. When the bars are the right height, tighten (cl) the expander bolt again. Always leave at least 2½ inches of the stem inside the headset; on many stems there is a line marking this limit.

Drop bar bent in (Rd bike) You've taken a spill, right? You are scraped and shook up, but OK. The bike is OK too, except that one of the handlebars has a new bend in it, so that it toes in. When you stop shaking, put the bike on its side so that the still-straight bar is flat on the ground. Step on the drop portion of the straight bar (careful, don't break the brake lever) and pull firmly upward on the folded bar.

ILLUSTRATION **3-2**
Straightening a Bent
Drop Bar

If the bars are aluminum, you might be able to get them straight enough to ride. Steel bars are a lot harder to bend. And any bar that has been bent and unbent is weak, so when you get a chance, get a replacement.

To replace handlebars (all bikes), first get the grip, tape, brake lever, horn, or whatever off the old ones. If you have lotsa trouble removing old handgrips, take the bike to a gas station with a shop, ask them if you can use the cleaning nozzle on their shop air hose, then stick the nozzle in the hole at the end of one handgrip, put your thumb over the hole in the other grip, and blast air pressure into the handlebars. Nine times out of ten the grips will both come loose and slide right off. For that tenth tough grip, use a razor knife and lotsa care to cut it off. Then loosen (c-cl) the binderbolt completely. Slide the bars out and take them to a shop. Get ones that are the same diameter at the stem or a little smaller. If you get smaller ones, find the correct size shim to make the new bars fit the stem. Don't get bars that are much too big for your stem — they will stretch and weaken the stem. On a mountain bike, if the bars are just a hair too big, you can do a neat trick to open up the stem if you have the kind of binderbolt that screws into a threaded hole. Take the binderbolt all the way out, turn it into the threaded hole from the back side, stick a penny into the slot there, and tighten (cl) the backwards binderbolt up against the penny to spread the stem opening a little. [See Illustration 4-1.]

Tape worn or unwound (Rd bike) Take the plugs out of the ends of the bars. If there is a screw in the middle of the plug, unscrew (c-cl) it until it is loose, then push it in and work the plug out. If your plugs don't have screws, just yank them out. Unwind the old tape completely. Get new tape. I recommend either cloth, thin leather, or the rubbery, stretchy type of plastic tape that is thicker in the middle than at the edges. You can use the extra-thick tape, or you can put on several layers of standard tape for a softer feel on your bars, but it can get to the point where you are out of touch with that zingy responsiveness of your bike's front end. Start wrapping the tape about 3 inches out from the midpoint of the bar where it is held by the stem. If the tape has no gum on it, you can stick the end down with a little piece of Scotch tape. Whichever type of tape you use, start by wrapping a couple turns in one place to cover the tape end. As you lay the tape on, keep it tight, and make it go directly from the roll to the bar. There's less to get tangled up that way. Overlap at least a third at all points. At the bends, you have to overlap more on the inside than on the outside. Just make sure it overlaps enough on the outside of the bend. Angle the tape across the bar behind the hand lever, making sure it is tight all the time. [See Illustration 3-3.] You can fold the hood up on most hand levers, so you can wrap tape close around the lever's post. At the end of the bar, leave a little tape to tuck in under the plug. (By the way, you can tuck things in there if you're traveling or cross-

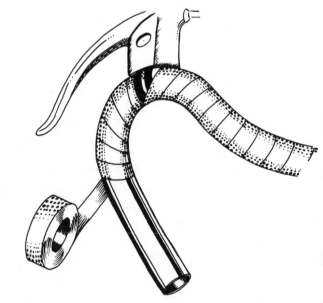

ILLUSTRATION **3-3**
Drop Bar Taping

ing borders, although I've heard that border guards have learned about that trick.) When you've finished taping and tucking, push and knock the plug back in with your hands. Don't use a hammer; it will mash the tape in two and you'll have to start all over. If you have tape left over, you can wrap it around the top tube of the frame where the handlebars hit if they are swung all the way around. Or you can put a little over the hole at the top end of your seat post, if you have a post with a hole at the top. Or you can use a little on a leaky vacuum cleaner hose, or a noisy kid's mouth, or a cracked pump handle. Sometimes I feel like my whole mish-mosh life is held together by old scraps of handlebar tape and used bike inner tubes.

STEM

4
Stem

(cl) means clockwise, and usually tightens a bolt or nut.
(c-cl) means counterclockwise, and usually loosens.

DESCRIPTION AND DIAGNOSIS: (all bikes) The stem, or gooseneck, as it is sometimes called, is a curved or angled piece of aluminum or chrome-moly tubing, one end of which holds the handlebars, the other end of which fits inside the headset. The stem holds the bars in a binding clamp which is tightened onto the bars by means of a short binderbolt. [See Illustration 4-1.] The end of the stem which sticks down into the head tube of the frame rotates freely, turning the front wheel back and forth, because it is not attached to the frame tube directly but to the steering column, which comes up from the fork. [See Illustration 8-1.] The bottom of the stem is held inside that steerer by means of a long expander bolt that either expands the diameter of the bottom of the stem or wedges it until it is jammed tight against the surrounding steering column.

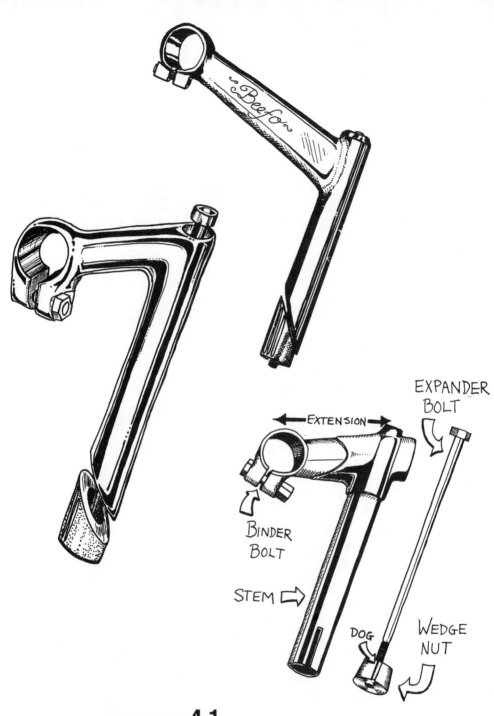

ILLUSTRATION 4-1
Road and Mountain Bike Stems

(Rd bike) Some of you road bike owners might wonder why your handlebars are so low. You might be tempted to raise the stem up. Don't. The top of the stem should be slightly lower than the top of the seat. (If the seat is sticking way up in the air, the problem is not the stem, but that the frame is too small.) Do you find the bent-over riding position uncomfortable? Maybe you would be happier on a mountain bike. The low position of the bars and the shortness of the stem on long-distance road bikes keep you bent over so you don't destroy your sitzplatz. OK? Just try riding a hundred miles or so on a bike that keeps you sitting upright, and you'll see what I mean. The bent-over riding position also increases your pedaling power and decreases your wind resistance. The Wright brothers, who knew a lot about wind resistance, invented the bent-over riding position. There *can* be problems with stem extension, however. You may find that, as you ride, either your knees are almost hitting the handlebars, or you have to stretch out so far to reach the bars that your arms and back ache all the time. First make sure you have the right frame size and seat position [see *Frame* and *Seat* chapters].

If your frame is the right size and your seat is set up right, you might have the wrong length extension on your stem. [See Illustration 4-1.] There is no rigid formula for stem extension. The formulas I have seen are absurdly complicated. Find a stem you can live with, and get accustomed to it. Ride more and worry less about the stem extension — that's my advice. If you decide to get a new stem with a different extension, see *Stem replacement* below.

PROBLEMS: *Stem loose or crooked* (all bikes) Your stem isn't held in tight, so that your handlebars turn independently of your front wheel. Or your stem is crooked. You crooked stem people may be riding straight down the road, but your handlebars are aiming off to one side. Or your handlebars are aiming straight down the road, but your bike just insists on going into the ditch. You've got to straighten up and tighten up. Go around to the front of the bike and hold the wheel between your legs. (Don't get kinky with it — just hold it.) Grasp the handlebars firmly with both hands and straighten them so that the stem extension lines up with the front wheel. (What's that? You can't straighten the bars? Loosen the expander bolt [see Illustration 4-1] two full turns. Then tap down on its head with a hammer so that the stem comes unwedged. Now straighten the handlebars.) Tighten up (cl) on the long expander bolt. An expander bolt should be tight enough to hold the stem, but not too tight. Try twisting the bars again. If they don't slip unless you pull quite hard, then the expander bolt is tight enough. The expander bolt should not be so tight that the stem can't slip if you crash. If you fall on the bars, you want *them* to give, not you. So don't tighten up on the expander bolt too much.

You have a little **crack** in your stem (all bikes). *Don't* ride with a cracked stem, especially if yours is an alloy one, or a welded steel one. Replace it! Now! No kidding — it's a terrible way to crash, having your stem break off.

To replace a stem, or to install a different stem if you have been referred here from above, you have to take the tape and brake lever off one end of the handlebar (see **Brake Hand Lever Slippage** if your lever is hard to get off), then loosen (c-cl) the short binderbolt [see Illustration 2-3] and slide the handlebar out of the stem. To release the expander bolt, unscrew (c-cl) it about two full turns, so that the head of the bolt rises up off the stem. Then take a hammer in one hand, hold onto the stem firmly with the other hand, and lightly tape the head of the expander downward with the hammer. It shouldn't take much to get the stem loose. Take it to the shop and match a new one. Also get a roll of handlebar tape or a new grip if you need one. Most stems are nearly the same diameter where they fit into the fork tube, but there are a number of different handlebar diameters. If you have to get a stem with a handlebar clamp that's too big for your bars, you can get a little sleeve of metal, called a shim (or sometimes a ferrule) that will fill the gap. But if your bars are too big to fit in your new stem, change the stem. Don't stretch the clamp on the stem. It might break. When your bars are back in the stem [see *Handlebars*], push *at least* 2½ inches of the stem down into the headset. If the stem fits so snugly into the tube down inside the headset that you can't push it down, loosen the big locknut that's on top of the headset [see Illustration 5-2]. This will let the tube loose a tiny bit, so the stem will slip down in. Now you need to straighten and tighten your stem, so turn to that section above. Then replace the brake lever [see *Brake Hand Lever*] and put on new handebar tape [see *Handlebars*].

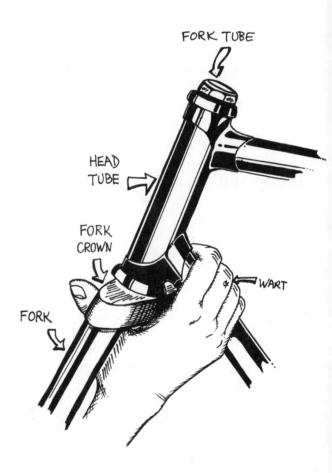

FORK TUBE

HEAD TUBE

FORK CROWN

FORK

WART

ILLUSTRATION **5-1**
Holding Fork
in Headset

5

Headset

(cl) means clockwise, and usually tightens a bolt or nut.
(c-cl) means counterclockwise, and usually loosens.

DESCRIPTION: (all bikes) The headset holds the front fork of the bike to the frontmost or "head" tube of the frame. [See Illustration 5-1.] A steering column comes up from the fork through the frame and is held in the headset bearings. The top of the steerer comes right up to the top of the head tube, so that you can stick the stem down into it and steer. There are a lot of parts around that steering column. [See Illustration 5-2.] Starting right at the crown of the fork, there is the fork crown bearing race, then the bearings, then the bottom set race, then the head tube, then the top set race, then the top threaded race (removable by unscrewing), then a washer (sometimes threaded and screwed up tight against the threaded race), and finally, on top, a big locknut. Some mountain bikes have oversize headsets to accommodate larger, strong-yet-light steering columns. These headsets work just like their smaller cousins, but if you have to get parts, go to a bike shop that caters to custom mountain bikes.

PROBLEMS: *Headset loose* (all bikes) The front of the bicycle clanks when you go over bumps. If you get off the bike and lift the front wheel off the ground and drop it, there is a clank. The fork seems loose in relation to the rest of the frame. Any of these very common symptoms tell you the same thing. Either your front wheel is loose, or your headset is loose. Check the wheel to make sure. Let the bike sit normally on the ground and see if you can wiggle the front wheel back and forth with your fingers, either on its bearings or in the fork. If the wheel is loose, see *Hubs,* page 103. If the front wheel is solid, that clanking you've noticed is due to a loose headset. There are very few headsets that will stay tight forever, so you should get used to tightening yours every year or so.

To tighten your headset (all bikes), first loosen the locknut, which is the topmost big nut of the headset. [See Illustration 5-2.] If there is a threaded washer under the locknut, loosen it, too. Tighten (cl) the top threaded bearing race, which is the next thing under the locknut that has some gripping surface on it. The threaded race might have flat outer surfaces like a nut, or a cross-hatch pattern that you're supposed to be able to grip with your bare hands. If your threaded race has flat surfaces so that it looks like a big nut, you're in luck. Use a huge crescent wrench if you have one, or a Ford monkey wrench if you can find one, or a channel lock wrench, or a vise-grip or even a pipe wrench if you don't mind chewing the thing up a bit. Jiggle and turn the handlebars as you tighten (cl) the threaded race, to make sure everything is seated in the headset. You shouldn't put much torque (twist) on the threaded race; you don't want it so tight that it squeezes the bearings. The idea is to tighten

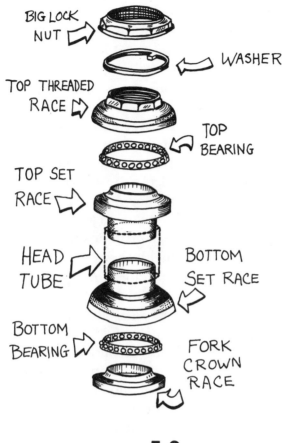

BIG LOCK NUT

WASHER

TOP THREADED RACE

TOP BEARING

TOP SET RACE

HEAD TUBE

BOTTOM SET RACE

BOTTOM BEARING

FORK CROWN RACE

ILLUSTRATION **5-2**
Headset, Exploded View

the bearings enough so that nothing rattles, but not so tight that the headset doesn't rotate smoothly.

Test for rattles by lifting the front wheel 2 inches off the ground and dropping it. If you have to turn the threaded race around and around before you can get rid of the clank, the little ball bearings have probably fallen out, due to excessive headset looseness. Naughty you! You should have done this adjustment *long* ago. Turn to the **overhaul** procedure two pages below, and rebuild your headset with new ball bearings.

When you have the adjustment just right, bring the washer back down on top of the threaded race. If your model has a threaded washer, that washer now has to be locked against the threaded race. This kind of threaded washer has notches in it. Use a curve and hook spanner [see *Tools*] or set a screwdriver into a notch, aiming clockwise, so that you can tap the screwdriver and drive the lockwasher down tight. Do it gently. You don't want to mess up the bearing surfaces. Screw the big top locknut down (cl) until it is snug. Try tightening down on it, using a bottom bracket spanner like the one on page 20 if you can get one, or a big crescent, or the Ford monkey wrench, or, if you can't do better, the channel lock wrench.

If tightening the big top locknut tightens the threaded bearing race at all, *stop tightening*. Your bearings are at stake. If the threaded bearing race is getting tight, hold onto the top locknut with one wrench, and back (c-cl) the threaded race off the bearings with a second wrench. This tightens the threaded race up against the top locknut, which is what you want. The two-wrench method is the best, if you can get two wrenches that big. You can use the vise-grip on the threaded race, if you don't clamp down too hard, but don't use a vise-grip on the top locknut — it is too easy to squish out of shape. If you have a lot of trouble with the tools you can get hold of, don't knock yourself out or mash up the threaded race or the big top locknut in the process. Take the bike to a good shop. They will have the right tools to do the job.

Headset stiff or sticky (all bikes) You find it difficult to steer your bicycle, or, when you steer, ugly crackling or grinding noises come out of the headset. Or when you are riding down a bumpy hill and put on your brakes, all kinds of cracking noises come from the headset. For any of these symptoms, first determine where the problem actually is. Take the front wheel off the bike [see **Wheel Removal,** page

96]. To make sure that the wheel isn't actually the trouble, hold the ends of the axle in your hands and spin the wheel. Does the axle tug and jerk in your hands or slip back and forth in the hub? If so, you have wheel hub trouble. If the wheel glides evenly on its axle, you can assume the trouble is in the headset. Just to make sure, check the stem where it fits down in the headset. Are there a good 2½ inches of the stem sticking down into the fork tube? If the stem wiggles at all when you push it back and forth, go to the *Stem* chapter and see if you can't take care of your noisy front end with some stem tightening. It isn't the stem? The problem must be the headset.

The headset might need adjusting and lubrication. The bearings might be dirty and worn. The races might be misshapen, or, worse, the frame might be misshapen in such a way that the races don't mount parallel to each other. Start with lubrication and adjustment. Follow the procedure for a loose headset, then lay the bike on its side and drop some oil down into the bearings. Does that help? No? Ah, well, can't win 'em all. If your headset needs more than oil and adjusting, it needs a complete overhaul. So have at it.

Start the *headset overhaul* by laying the bike down on its left side with a clean white rag under the headset (bearings are easier to find on white rags). Loosen (c-cl) the expander bolt that's on top of the stem two full turns, then tap the bolt head with a hammer to unwedge the stem inside the fork tube [see Illustration 4-1]. Twist and pull the handlebars to get the stem out. If you have enough brake and gear cable slack, turn the handlebars to one side and lash one end to the down tube with an old inner tube or something. Remove the front wheel if you haven't already. Now you can start dismantling the headset. [See Illustration 5-2.] Use a big wrench to take the big top locknut off and put it in a can or paper cup where you won't lose it. Take the washer off and put it in the same place, and the cable hanger if you have one. Before you take the top threaded bearing race off, think a minute. That threaded race is the only thing left holding the fork tube in the frame. When you undo it, the fork tube will want to slip and flop around, sending ball bearings all over the place. So, to keep things simple, leave the bike lying on its side, and hold the fork up against the frame with one hand while you loosen (c-cl) the top threaded race with the other hand.

As the top threaded race spins its way up the fork tube, you will begin to see one of three things. Either a number of big ball bearings will start falling out from under the top threaded race, or another inset race will appear with tiny bearings falling out of it, or you will see ball bearings held in a retainer, a neat little metal ring that fits around them. Everybody, take the top threaded race all the way off the fork tube, still holding the fork in place in the frame with one hand. Get all the ball bearings out of the top threaded race and the top set race. If they aren't in a retainer, count them. How many are there? Write that down, here _____ so you won't forget. There are so many different kinds of headsets, all with different numbers of bearings, that I can't tell you how many bearings your head-set should have. Collect all the bearings and put them in your container with the other headset parts. If your headset is the kind with the tiny bearings and the inset race, take the inset race off and put it into the container, too.

Make sure the fork crown end of the headset is over the white rag, and draw the fork out. Bearings will come raining down on the rag. Count them. Get any that are stuck with grease to the race or the fork tube or the frame or your nose, and put all the bearings in the container. (If you have an inset bearing race, put it in too.)

Take the fork crown bearing race (the bottom-most one) off the fork tube. If it is stuck to the fork, take a screwdriver and gently pry it free, working your way around and around it, prying just a little at a time. You don't want to bend or scar that thing. When you get it off, hold it a second and look at it. If you have the inset bearing races with the tiny bearings, you will notice that the fork crown race is very similar to the inset races. Can you see the difference? That's right. The inset races have curved outer surfaces, and the fork crown has a flat outer surface. Now that you know and see the difference, you can put both races together in the container.

Whether or not you have the inset bearing races, you will have two large races that are set (hence the name set races) into the frame of the bike. Look at them. If they sit flush against the frame all the way around, leave them alone. If not, they may be bent or the frame may be bent. The races are easier to replace than the frame, so hope it's the races. To take bent races out, twist them back and forth with your hands. If they turn, take them out with your hands. If they are too tight to get out with your hands, stick a foot-long piece of pipe or the big screwdriver down the frame tube. With the bike still on its side, put one end of the pipe or screwdriver into the frame tube and slide it all the way in until it stops against the lip of the bearing race at the other end. Lift the end of the pipe or screwdriver that's

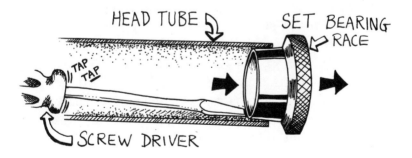

ILLUSTRATION **5-3**
Tapping Out a Set Race

sticking out of the frame tube, so it goes through the frame tube diagonally. Get a friend to hold the frame while you gently tap the thing with a small hammer. (A friend is an incredibly useful aid which I failed to mention in the tool section. Get one at least.) Work around and around the race, gently tapping as you go. When it pops out, take it to your favorite bike shop for replacement.

If your set races are not bent, clean them with solvent. If you're not in a hurry, put some solvent in the container with all the other headset parts, and go do something for a while, like take a walk with your friend. If you're rushed, take a rag with some solvent on it and wipe off all the parts, especially the bearings and races. When all of the bearing surfaces are really clean, take a good look at them. You might even use a magnifying glass. Are the balls dent-free? Is the shiny path in the race where the balls were running smooth, and the same color all the way round? Is that shiny path round? Put the races down on a flat surface, like a formica table. Do they sit perfectly flat? If the answer to any of these questions is no, buy new parts. If you aren't sure, take them to someone who knows the difference between good bearings and shot bearings. Take the old bearings to the store and match them to get *exact* replacements. (Fancy-type headsets are often too thick for the short fork tubes on standard bikes.) Get a new fork, too, if your old one is bent. If you have a mountain bike with an oversize steering column, go to a shop that caters to that kind of bike to get replacement parts. Whatever replacing you do, get a few extra ball bearings for spares. If you get a new headset, make sure that the threads and the lockwasher are the same as your old one and that the whole set is the correct size.

You can start **reassembling the headset** when you have clean and/or new headset parts. Remember, frame lying on its side, clean white rag under the head tube. Clean out the head tube, then put the two set races (top and bottom) into it (unless you never took them out). The one with the bigger cup cover is the bottom one. Put a block of wood on each race and tap it home with a hammer if it's a little tight. Check all around the races and make sure they are flush against the frame. When they are, slip the fork crown race down over the fork tube till it's down flush on the crown. [See Illustration 5-2.] That may take a little hammer-and-block treatment, but be very careful, as that little race can bend easily. Tap gently, round and round the race. Fill the grooves of both set races with grease. (If you have the tiny bearings and insets, fill both insets with grease.) Stick the ball bearings in the grease of the bottom set race (or inset) only. Remember how many there's supposed to be? If not, look back a couple pages to where you wrote it down.

If your ball bearings are in a retainer, you don't have to count them and stick them carefully in the grease. You lucky dog. Just make sure the retainer goes in right, so the solid outer ring does *not* rub against the race.

When the bearings are all in, wipe off extra grease. You don't want extra grease slopping out of the works because it attracts sand and grit, the archenemies of bearings. Clean off the fork and hold it in one hand. Hold the frame still with the other. Carefully guide the fork tube up through the head tube of the frame. (If you have the insets, take one of them and slip the fork tube through it until the inset rests on the crown race, then slip the fork into the head tube.)

When the fork tube is up snug, rotate it back and forth, holding it firmly in place. Roll easily? It better. If not, take it apart and have another look at things. If it feels nice (good bearings *do* feel nice — it's worth the work), hold the fork up in the frame with one hand, and with the other stick the bearings in the grease in the top set race. Does it seem ridiculous doing this one-handed? Well, persevere. Or get a friend to hold the fork in. But if you're working with un-retained ball bearings, don't let that fork loose. With all the ball bearings in place — and still holding the fork — screw (cl) on the top threaded race. Start it very carefully on the threads at the top of the fork tube. A lot of threads get ruined at this point, and if it should happen to you, you'll have to take the fork out, take it to a good bike shop and get it threaded, then go through the whole ball bearing procedure again. So start that threaded bearing race carefully. Screw it all the way down (cl) just snug against the bearings. Now you can stop holding the fork still. Try twisting it back and forth. It should be smooth, even if the threaded race is down pretty tight. If it's tight in some places and loose in others, something is wrong. Check the set races and the crown race to make sure they are flush against the frame or fork. You might have bent frame or fork problems, in which case you should turn to those chapters. You may just want to live with it, but try to remember that it's not a good idea to run into curbs. If everything looks and feels good, turn back to **tighten your headset** to adjust the bearings. Finish up by replacing the wheel and resetting the brakes. Your bike should steer as smooth as a Rolls Royce now.

6
Fork

(cl) means clockwise, and usually tightens a bolt or nut.
(c-cl) means counterclockwise, and usually loosens.

DESCRIPTION: (all bikes) The thing that holds your front wheel to the rest of the bike. Starting at the top, the fork has a long tube or steering column, which can't be seen from the outside because it is inside the headset and the head tube of the bike frame. At the lower end of the steering column there is often a visible fork crown, into which two blades or "arms" are brazed. [See Illustration 6-1.] On some models, the crown and the two blades of the fork are all one piece of solid metal. On other models, like the uni-crown style, the fork blades are curved in at the top and brazed or welded directly to the steering column. Still other forks have two-piece crowns, into which the blades are clamped and/or glued. Each style has its good and bad points; strong forks are made in all of the different styles.

At the ends of the fork blades, there are little upside-down U-shaped ends, called drop-outs, because that's where

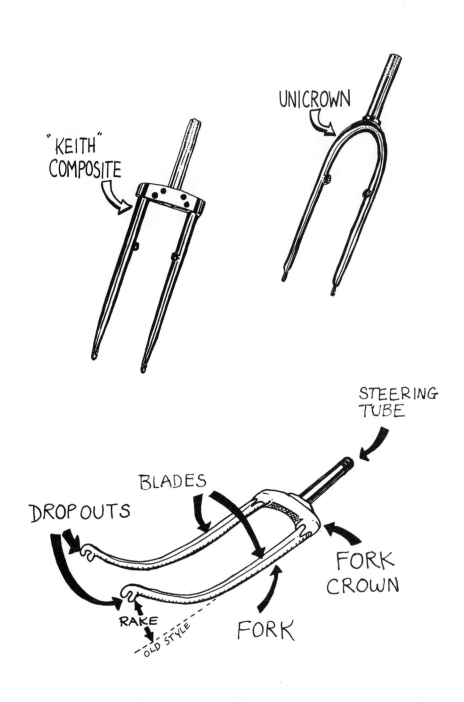

"KEITH" COMPOSITE

UNICROWN

STEERING TUBE

BLADES

DROPOUTS

FORK CROWN

RAKE

OLD STYLE

FORK

ILLUSTRATION **6-1**
Forks

the wheel drops out. Just hope the wheel doesn't until you want it to. The wheel axle fits into the drop-outs and should be held firmly there.

Forks are important. So when you get a bike, get one with the best forks you can afford. That doesn't mean the beefiest, heaviest forks. Big beefy forks may be strong in some cases, but they are often so rigid that if you hit a curb hard, or go into a culvert, your whole bike frame is likely to self-destruct. And the impact delivered to you will be pretty destructive too. Not that lighter forks will always save you. They just give you a much better chance because they flex. You hit something, and they do a good job of absorbing the shock. They can be straightened or replaced a lot more easily than the frame, or you. OK?

Forks come with a great variety of crowns, and a great variety of bends, including straight. The variations affect the stiffness of the forks. The stronger the crown and blade, and the steeper the fork blade (i.e., the less deflection), the stiffer the fork. A straight fork can be flexible, if the tubing is light and flexy, and the blades are deflected forward from the crown. Stiff forks hold the road best and waste less of the rider's energy through flexing. Flexible forks give a more comfortable ride, and some people like the springy feeling they give. Take your pick. Some racers like stiff forks. Mountain bikers like strong forks, but some prefer forks with a little flex. Touring people usually prefer more flexible forks.

PROBLEMS: *Fork bent* (all bikes) Don't try to straighten it yourself! You might wind up with a dangerously misshapen fork. Take the whole bike to a reliable shop and ask if the fork is worth trying to straighten. They should have nifty tools and much know-how that can straighten minor bends. Replace a fork that is bent so much that the front wheel hits the frame, or any fork on which the paint just below the crown bubbled and cracked. New forks don't cost so much that you should take the risk of using a bent and rebent one. Metal that has been bent and rebent is weak — fatigued. It might give up on you when you need it most. Imagine yourself going very fast with, and then without, a front wheel. Got the picture?

To remove and replace a fork, follow the **Headset Overhaul** procedure, page 85. Check the headset while you're at it. Make sure the steering column on your new fork is the same length as your old one. Take the old fork to the shop and have them match it.

7
Wheels

(cl) means clockwise, and usually tightens a bolt or nut.
(c-cl) means counterclockwise, and usually loosens.

DESCRIPTION AND DIAGNOSIS: (all bikes) The round things. Each has an axle, a hub with bearings, spokes, spoke nipples, a rim, a rim strip, a tire, and a tube. The wheel is attached to the fork either by two big nuts on the axle, or by a quick-release lever, a handy gadget, which should always be on the left side of the bike, and locked firmly in such a position that the end of the lever points diagonally up and to the rear of the bike.

On the rear wheel of a multi-speed mountain or road bike, there is a cluster of sprockets on the right side of the hub. On 3-speed cruiser bikes, the rear wheel has a cable and chain (called the indicator) going into one end of the axle. [See Illustration 10-30.] On 1-speed cruisers, there is a metal bracket that drops down and forward from the left side of the rear axle and clamps onto the frame (that's your coaster brake arm).

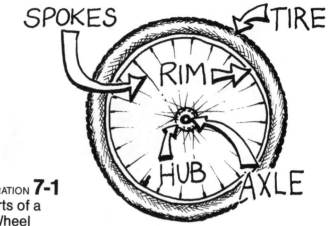

ILLUSTRATION **7-1**
Parts of a
Wheel

What you have to do most often to wheels is take them off and put them on — to do all kinds of things. [See **Wheel Removal** and **Wheel Replacement** in this chapter, and read the paragraphs that talk about your kind of bike.]

If your wheel is loose (the rear one rubs the frame if it is loose), or it doesn't spin smoothly and/or makes nasty noises, see **Hubs** in this chapter.

If your rim wobbles side to side while you slowly revolve the wheel (or you notice it while you're riding), see **Spokes and Rims** in this chapter.

WHEEL REMOVAL
(cl) means clockwise, and usually tightens a bolt or nut.
(c-cl) means counterclockwise, and usually loosens.

(all bikes) First you have to get the wheels off the ground while you work on them. That will keep the bike from falling on its tender parts when you pull a wheel out from underneath it. It's a good idea to hang it up somehow — from an auto carrier rack, hooks, a rope over a tree limb, or just a plain floor stand [see page 26]. If all else fails, have your neighborhood Atlas hold it up. The more firmly the bike is held, the better. If you can't hang the bike up, lay it gently on its left side, and on some surface that won't scratch it up. Or if you have a cruiser without any tender levers on the handlebars, you can stand the bike upside down on its handlebars and seat. Just remember that in the directions, "down" means down the way the bike normally rides, so for you upside-down people, "down" means up. Perfectly clear. OK, now you've got the bike in position.

(Mt bike, Rd bike) If you are *removing a rear wheel* from a road bike or mountain bike, shift into the highest gear to move the chain into the smallest rear sprocket on the gear cluster.

(3-speed cruiser) If you are *removing a 3-speed rear wheel,* put it in high gear and find the little chain and pole that come out of the right side of the rear hub [called the indicator — see Illustration 10-30]. Loosen (cl) the little knurled locknut on the indicator pole, and completely unscrew (c-cl) the sleeve that's attached to the cable that goes to the hand lever. Take that loose cable end and stick it somewhere out of the way.

(1-speed cruiser) If you are going to remove a rear wheel from a coaster brake cruiser, you have to undo the brake arm bracket from the bike frame. Go to the left side of the wheel and look at the thick metal arm that sticks forward along the bike frame from the hub. See the little bracket that holds the end of that arm in place? Unscrew (c-cl) the bolt and nut that hold the bracket tight around the frame tube. When the bracket is detached from the brake arm, put the bolt back into its bracket hole and screw (cl) the nut onto it, so those two little parts don't get lost.

(all bikes) If the wheel has hand brakes, you might have to release them. Look down on the brake shoes from straight above. If they are far enough away from the rim that the tire will fit between them, or if you have a pump handy and can let the air out of the tire and pump it back up when you have finished replacing the wheel, *don't touch the brakes.* If it even looks like the wheel can squeeze out through the brakes, skip ahead to "ready to take the wheel off," because you are. But if you are going to have lots of trouble getting the rim or the tire past the brake shoes, you have to release the brakes.

(Mt bike) For the *release of center-pull brakes,* you may have a transverse cable that you can unhook from one of the arms of the brake mechanism. [See Illustrations 2-11 and 2-12.] The barrels on the ends of the short transverse cable fit into prongs on the brake arms. If you squeeze the brake shoes against the rim with a third hand tool, or even with your own second hand, you can simply pull the barrel end of the transverse cable out of its prong, and the brake will be released. If you have a center-pull brake that is activated by a cam plate and rollers, squeeze the brake shoes in as described above, then twist the cam plate sideways to release the brake. (If you need help on brake releasing, see *Center-Pull Mechanism,* page 49.)

(Rd bike) *Releasing side-pull brakes* is usually done by turning a lever on the brake mechanism at the anchor bolt [see Illustration 2-9]. This takes tension off the cable, and lets the brake shoes move far enough apart to let the tire past.

(3-speed cruiser) *Releasing the brakes* may be easier at the brake hand lever end of the system [see Illustration 2-1], especially if the bike is a 3-speed. Apply the third hand tool to your brake shoes, or just have a friend grab the brake shoes and squeeze them against the rim. The cable will now be loose. Push the looseness in the cable backwards through the housing to the brake hand lever. At the lever, pull the cable housing away from the brake lever post and see if there is a slot that will allow you to pull the cable down out of the post. If there is no such slot in the lever trunk, there should be one where the cable end is attached to the hand lever. If nothing else works, loosen (c-cl) the cable anchor bolt at the brake mechanism [see Illustrations

2-9, 2-11, and 2-12], but don't let the cable slip all the way out of the anchor bolt if you can help it.

(all bikes) You are now ready to *release the wheel.* See what's holding the wheel axle to the frame. If there are big nuts or wing nuts around the axle, loosen the nut at each end of the axle (c-cl). It is best if you use two wrenches, so that you are loosening at both ends at once. Remember that when you turn the nuts on both ends of the axle counterclockwise, you will be turning them opposite directions. What? How can that be? It's because each nut, being on an opposite end, has an opposite perspective. It's like the writing on your T-shirt looks funny in the mirror. Anyway, take my word for it; the nuts *do* unscrew in opposite directions.

(Mt bike, Rd bike) If your wheel is held not by nuts but by a lever on one end of the axle and a smooth, cone-shaped nut on the other end, you have a *quick-release* device. It is a wonderful gizmo. To free the wheel, all you have to do is pull the lever loose.

(all bikes) Now everybody is ready to *remove the wheel.* If it's a front wheel, they come out so easily that it has probably already dropped out of the slots (drop-outs) in the frame that held it. If not, just pull diagonally down and forward. Rear wheels also have to be pulled down and forward out of the drop-outs, but the chain will complicate things a little. With cruiser bikes, go ahead and pull the wheel out of the frame, and then just lift the chain off the sprocket by hand if you need to. On a road bike, first make sure the chain is on the smallest sprocket. Then stand at the rear of the bike and ease the rear wheel down and forward with your left hand while you pull the derailleur (changer) back with your right hand. The small sprocket should then slip by the changer, and you can wiggle the wheel fore and aft a bit to free the sprocket from the chain. Don't force things. Let them come easily. With any luck you can get that wheel off without touching the messy chain.

WHEEL REPLACEMENT

(cl) means clockwise, and usually tightens a bolt or nut.
(c-cl) means counterclockwise, and usually loosens.

If you have gotten your wheel off already, I assume you know what kind of device holds it to the drop-outs. Whatever kind of wheel it is, remember that any washers usually go *outside* the drop-outs.

(Mt bike, Rd bike) If you are ***putting in a back wheel with a quick-release lever,*** loosen (c-cl) the lever a few turns, holding the cone end in one hand, and the lever in the other. Put the right gear control lever all the way forward (the way it is when you're in high gear). Now work your wheel into the drop-outs, slipping the chain over the smallest sprocket on the sprocket cluster. Set the quick-release lever so it is open (pointing straight out) and tighten up (cl) the quick-release device until both the cone and the lever ends are finger tight against the frame. Pull the wheel toward the rear of the bike until the right end of the axle seats against a block in the drop-out. Keep the right end of the axle seated, and move the left side of the axle until the rim of the wheel is centered between the chain stays. Hold the wheel in place with one hand, and lock the quick-release lever closed. It should be pretty hard to push that lever all the way closed. If it isn't, unlock the lever, then hold the cone in one hand, and with the other hand tighten (cl) the lever about ½ turn. Align the wheel, and lock the lever closed again. Hard to lock this time? Good. Reset your brakes if they were released, and your wheel is ready for action.

(Mt bike, Rd bike) If you are ***putting in a front wheel with quick-release,*** make sure the lever is unlocked (pointing straight out), and slip the axle into the drop-outs. Seat the axle in the drop-outs, then tighten up (cl) and lock the quick-release lever. Check the wheel alignment to make sure the rim is centered between the fork blades. If it is off center, you may need to tighten all the spokes on one side of the wheel (see page 116). If it is really cockeyed, so the tire is hitting one of the fork blades, you may have a bent fork. See page 94.

(all bikes) To *replace a rear wheel with bolt-on axle,* first spin (c-cl) the nuts out to the ends of the axle. If you have a multi-speed bike, put your gear control lever in high gear.

(Cruisers) One-speed people, put the chain on the sprocket, slide the axle into the drop-outs, then attach the thick metal brake arm to the bike's frame with the bracket. Just hand tighten (cl) the bolt and nut for now, so you can move the bracket back and forth on the frame if needed. Center the wheel so the tire has equal room between the chainstays of the frame, then slide the wheel back so the chain is almost, but not quite, tight. Now, while holding the wheel in its centered position, tighten (cl) the axle nuts firmly. It may take a friend to do all those things at the same time. Pedal the bike and test the brakes. (If they are acting up, see page 29.) Also make sure the chain isn't either floppy or tighter than a banjo string. You want about ½ inch of up-and-down play in the chain if you grab it with your fingers (yuk!) halfway between the front and back sprockets.

(Cruisers) Three-speed people, put the chain on the sprocket, then work the axle into the drop-outs. You have to pull the wheel back until the chain has only ½ inch of up-and-down play, *and* at the same time you have to center (align) the rim of the wheel between the chain stays. With both of these conditions met, hold the wheel in exactly that position while you tighten (cl) the nuts against the frame. This could require a friend. Especially if the axle turns while you're tightening one nut, in which case you'll have to tighten both nuts at the same time. When you've got them fairly tight, and the chain slack and alignment both look good, start threading (cl) the indicator sleeve onto the indicator [see Illustration 10-30]. Make sure the control lever is in the high gear position, then screw (cl) the sleeve down until the cable has almost no slack. Lock up (c-cl) the lockring. Test the gears. Problems? See *Power Train, Hub Changer,* page 217.

(Mt bike, Rd bike) People with multi-speed derailleurs, work your wheel axle into the drop-outs, slipping the chain over the smallest sprocket. Seat both axles all the way into the ends of the drop-out slots and hand tighten (cl) the nuts. Keeping the right end of the axle firmly seated, slide the left end slightly forward until the front of the wheel is centered (aligned) between the two chain stays. With the wheel in exactly this position, tighten (cl) the nuts up well against the frame.

(all bikes) Whichever kind of rear wheel you have re-placed, tighten up the brakes. This means reversing the process you used to release them. Check them out. If they aren't working right, see the *Brakes* chapter for help.

To *replace a front wheel with a bolt-on axle,* spin (c-cl) the nuts until they're near the ends of the axle, then work the axle all the way into the drop-outs. Tighten (cl) both nuts with your fingers, then make sure both ends of the wheel axle are still seated all the way against the tops of the drop-out slots. Check the alignment by seeing if the rim of the wheel is equidistant from each of the fork blades. If it's way off center, like rubbing against one of the fork blades, your forks are badly bent out of alignment [see page 94]. If the wheel is just a bit to one side, you can "true" it over with the spokes (see page 116). Now tighten (cl) the axle nuts well with a wrench. If tightening one nut turns the whole axle, use a wrench on each nut. Recheck the align-ment, reset your brakes if they were released, and you are set to go.

HUBS

(cl) means clockwise, and usually tightens a bolt or nut.
(c-cl) means counterclockwise, and usually loosens.

DESCRIPTION: (all bikes) A hub consists of an axle, two bearing sets, a casing, and sometimes a quick-release lever [see Illustration 7-2]. If you can find no evidence of bearing sets on your hub, you have one with sealed cartridge bearings; you'll never have to adjust or oil it, you lucky stiff.

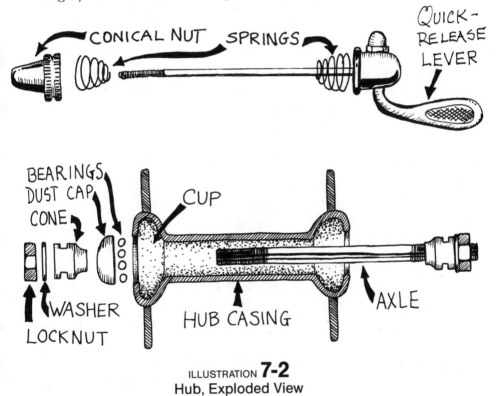

ILLUSTRATION **7-2**
Hub, Exploded View

If you have adjustable, or sealed adjustable bearings, though, each bearing set has a locknut, a washer that is kept from turning by a pin that fits into a groove in the axle, a cone, the ball bearings, and a bearing cup, which is pressed permanently into the hub casing. On some models there are no washers and locknuts. These models use the drop-outs (those slots in the frame) of the bike frame as a washer, and the big nut that holds the axle to the bike frame as a locknut.

If you have sealed adjustable bearings, you may notice a plastic seal that fits around the bearings snugly, in place of the dust cap [see Illustration 7-2]. There may be one or two little holes in this seal, and perhaps some "Open-Close" indicators with arrows. These indicate which way to twist the seal if you want to open it and squirt grease in, then close it to reseal the bearings.

PROBLEMS: **Loose wheel** (all bikes) Your wheel wiggles from side to side, or rubs the frame. Fix it now. Your bearings are at stake. First, see if the wheel is loose in the frame. If it is, you just need to tighten up your axle nuts or quick-release lever. [See **Wheel Replacement** above.] When the wheel holders are tight, grab the tire and see if you can still wiggle the wheel from side to side.

If the wheel still wiggles, your problem is **loose cones.** Depending on what kind of bike you have, see the paragraphs below that apply to it.

(Mt bike, Rd bike) If you have **quick-release** wheels, tightening the cones will take two spanners. You are going to have to work simultaneously on both ends of the axle, and that can get *confusing.* If you have a nut on each end of an axle and you want to loosen them both, you turn them both counterclockwise. That sounds simple enough. But you find yourself turning the wrenches in opposite directions. How can this be? Stand a tolerant friend directly in front of you, face to face, take your *right* foot and kick your friend in the shin. Notice that you've kicked his *left* shin. It's the same problem. It doesn't seem to make sense unless you take the time to look at each thing in its own perspective. Remember when following the directions that "clockwise" or "counterclockwise" are from the perspective of looking at the nut from the same end of the axle that the nut is on, not through the spokes from the opposite side.

But it's even more confusing than that. Each threaded end of the axle is going to have not one but two threaded parts on it, a cone and a locknut [see Illustration 7-3]. To screw or unscrew any one thing on the axle, you have to first go to the other end and tighten the two things there into each other. Then you can use one of them to hold the axle steady while you screw the thing you originally wanted to screw. Now all this sounds confusing, but it shouldn't prevent you from doing what you want to do. If you enjoy exercising yourself on mind bogglers, you can study Illustration 7-3 until you grasp "the concept." Or you can just make a point of following the directions very carefully, doing each step as you read it. Don't read the section like a newspaper, without looking at a bike, unless you want to blow your mind.

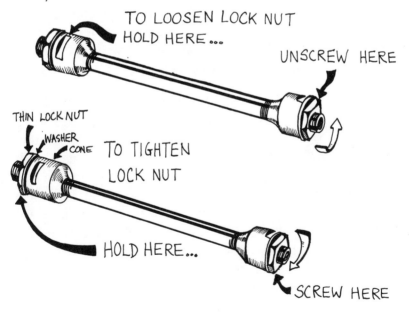

ILLUSTRATION **7-3**
Tightening and Loosening a Right Locknut

First check for looseness. Is either of the cone-washer-locknut sets loose, not locked together? Let's say the left one is loose. Put one spanner on the thin locknut on the right end of the axle, and tighten (cl) the left cone until it is snug against the bearings. Back the left cone off (c-cl) about ½ turn, or until the wheel spins easily. Then, still holding the spanner on the right thin locknut, tighten down the left thin locknut onto the left cone.

If this process tightens up the left cone on the bearings, put a spanner on the right cone, and back off (c-cl) the left thin locknut. Back the left cone off the bearings (c-cl), bring the left thin locknut in snug against the washer and cone, and do a two-spanner tighten, so the three left side parts are locked together well. Try the wheel. It has to spin smoothly but not wiggle from side to side. If it's too loose or too tight, take heart and try, try again. Sometimes it requires three spanners; one to hold the right side still, and the others to do a two-spanner tighten on the left end parts.

If no amount of patience will get the wheel so that it glides smoothly without being loose, you have bearing problems. See the hub overhaul procedure below.

(Cruisers) Look at the left side of any cruiser hub (on a coaster brake rear wheel, look at the *right* side instead). Starting at the left end of any axle, you should have first a big nut (sometimes a wing nut), then the drop-outs (the slot in the frame that holds the wheel), then a thin locknut, then a washer, then the cylindrical cone that disappears into the hub and has two slots at its outside edge for a thin spanner [see Illustration 7-2]. Your wheel may have no thin locknut. In that case, the big axle nut acts as a locknut. Think of it as such in this whole section, and do your adjustment with the wheel *on* the bike.

You *must* have a spanner that fits into the slots in the cones to work on your hub. Campagnolo makes a good set, if you can get them. But don't monkey with your hub unless you have a thin spanner that is of high quality, and fits.

Your hub may have a slotted cone on only one end of the axle. If so, don't monkey with the end that has no slot in its cone (the slotted cone should be on the left side, but this isn't always the case). Loosen (c-cl) only the left big axle nut. Tightening the cones should be done with the wheel held in place by the right big axle nut.

Get your thin spanner in the slots on the left cone, tighten (cl) the cone up on the bearings, back it off (c-cl) about ½ turn, until the wheel spins easily. Then tighten (cl) the left thin locknut (or big axle nut) down against the washer and cone. This may tighten up the cone on the bearings. If it does, use two spanners, one backing the left cone (c-cl) and one tightening (cl) the left thin locknut. When you have the cone and thin locknut set so that the wheel spins smoothly but doesn't wiggle from side to side, tighten (cl) the big nut. Spin the wheel, then ride the bike, to make sure the bearing is smooth. If it isn't or if it's making lots of weird crackly grinding noises, see the *hub overhaul* procedure below.

(Cruisers) To *adjust the bearings on the rear wheel* of a bike with coaster brakes, tighten (cl) the LEFT axle nut, then you can adjust the cone on the RIGHT side of the wheel, over there where the sprocket is [see Illustration 2-14]. Loosen (c-cl) the right axle nut, loosen (c-cl) the big locknut, tighten (cl) the cone down on the bearings with a cone wrench (it usually requires a special big cone wrench) and then back it off about ¼ turn. Then tighten (cl) both the big locknut and the big axle nut. Make sure the wheel spins freely, but without sloppy side-to-side play; a coaster brake hub can self-destruct if the bearings are either too loose or too tight.

(all bikes) To *overhaul a hub,* first remove the wheel from the bike. [See *Wheel Removal* for help.] If the wheel is a rear one from a 1-speed or 3-speed bike, take it to a good shop for overhaul — special tools and know-how are needed. If it is a rear wheel with a freewheel, go to *Rear Sprocket, remove the freewheel,* page 188. When you have removed the freewheel, you can treat the hub like a front wheel hub. If it is a rear wheel with many sprockets on a cassette, you don't have to remove them. Isn't that handy? If the wheel was held in the drop-outs by a quick-release lever, unscrew (c-cl) the lever, take the unit out of the wheel, then screw it (cl) together again so you don't lose those little springs.

For a short exposition on the subject of getting confused while working on both ends of an axle, turn back to page 104 and read the first paragraphs of *quick-release.* Start the overhaul by putting one thin spanner on the right cone, and another spanner on the right thin locknut (use the big axle nut as a locknut if your hub has no thin locknuts). Lock the right nut against the right cone and washer. From now on, you want that cone-washer-locknut set to stay put.

Lay the wheel down with the right end of the axle resting on a clean rag. Reach under the wheel and put a spanner on the right cone. Put another spanner on the left locknut and unscrew it (c-cl) all the way up off the axle. Now unscrew (c-cl) the left cone up off the end of the axle. Put the parts in a bowl as they come off.

If there is a dust cap, a ring of thin, often shiny metal pushed into a hub casing [see Illustration 7-2], pry it out gently with a screwdriver. Often, to get the dust cap out, you have to pick the wheel up and pull the axle down part way — *not* all the way, just far enough so you can slip a screwdriver into the axle hole in the dust cap and pry it out. Work around and around the dust cap as you pry, to keep from bending it.

If there is a seal rather than a dustcap, do *not* pry it out with any hard tool. If you can pull it out with your little finger, OK. Otherwise, leave it alone.

Count the bearings in the left side of the hub. Write the number here _____ . Do the bearings fill the cup completely? If there are big gaps between them, some are missing. There should be only a small amount of extra space between the bearings.

Hold the right end of the axle in the hub so the bearings on that side won't jump out and run away, then turn the wheel over and dump the left side bearings out. To complete the left side bearing dump, get a small magnet or a finger into the left cup and probe out any recalcitrant bearings. Put all the left side bearings in the bowl before they can run off and hide from you.

Turn the wheel back over on its right side and slide the axle out. Dump the right side bearings on the clean rag. Complete the bearing dump with a magnet or finger. Count the bearings and write the number here _____. If it's not the same number that you had on the left side, you're missing some bearings somewhere. Capture all the balls in the bowl. Remove the right side dust cap if there is one.

Clean all the parts in the bowl, and the cups that are in the hub; soak the parts in solvent. Examine all the bearing surfaces. Look closely at the shiny rings on the cones and cups where the balls roll. Are there rows of tiny pits? Are the ball bearings discolored? Do your balls have pitted patches? (Ouch!) Is the axle stripped of its threads in places? If you have to replace any of the hub parts, it is best to get a whole new set of cones, ball bearings, washers, locknuts, and axle. If you get new parts, lock one new cone-washer-locknut set on the new axle in exactly the same place the old axle had its right cone-washer-locknut set. Whatever replacement parts you get, try to match the brand name, and make sure the replacements are *identical* to the old ones. Get extra ball bearings for the ones that may run off and hide; they are shy little fellows; you have to figure on losing a few.

Begin the **hub reconstruction** by putting the right dust cap over the left end of the axle. Slide it down like a collar over the right cone, so that it will be in position to put in the right side of the hub casing. Remember that whatever you put into the hubs — bearings, grease, cones, etc. — has to be spotlessly clean. No water, grit, or solvent on it. Put the wheel down on its left side and spread light bicycle grease around in the right cup. Not too much. Extra grease attracts grit (you can use oil if you are fastidious and want the least possible friction, but oil has to be replenished frequently). Push the axle part way into the hub. Stick the right number of ball bearings in the grease around the inside of the cup. There should be only slight spaces between the ball bearings.

Slide the axle all the way into the hub until the right cone rests on the bearings. Push the right dust cap (if you have one) into the hub casing. Pick up the wheel and hold the axle in place as you turn the wheel over and rest it on the right end of the axle.

Put grease in the left cup and stick the right number of ball bearings in the grease. Screw the left cone down (cl) the axle until it is snug against the ball bearings. Push the dust cap into the left side of the housing. Put the left washer on the axle, and screw the left thin locknut on (cl). Pick up the wheel and give it a spin, holding the axle. If there is slippage back and forth on the axle, the ball bearings may be stacking up in the cups; the little buggers are still putting up a fight in there. Put the wheel down flat and jiggle and twist the axle until your balls get in line. Heh. Screw in (cl) the left cone until it is snug against the bearings, then back it off ½ turn and tighten (cl) the locknut against it. Remember the bearings should be tight enough that there is no wiggle, but loose enough that the wheel spins freely.

If it's a rear hub for a freewheel, put some oil or plumbers' thread goop (like Never-seez) on the threads and replace the freewheel carefully, making *sure* you don't strip the threads. If it is a quick-release hub, stick the pole of the unit with a spring around it into the left end of the axle. Put the other spring on the cone end of the quick-release pole, and screw (cl) the cone onto the pole. The narrow ends of the quick-release springs should point toward the center of the hub.

Replace the wheel in the drop-outs. Align your nice smoothly running wheel. If big axle nuts hold the wheel and act as locknuts too, check the cone adjustment when the big nuts are tight. Loosen the left cone if necessary. Whew! Your wheel rolls smooth now. Spin it a time or two. What a marvel of free-flow it is now! Well worth the trouble.

SPOKES AND RIMS

(cl) means clockwise, and usually tightens a bolt or nut.
(c-cl) means counterclockwise, and usually loosens.

DESCRIPTION: (all bikes) Spokes are the lacy wires that miraculously hold the thin metal rim in a round shape. The spokes are stuck through holes in the flanges of the hub; these holes are often beveled to accommodate the curve of the spoke at its head end. The bevel or countersink of each spoke hole in the hub is *not* for the head of the spoke to settle down into. It is for the curve of the spoke. The head

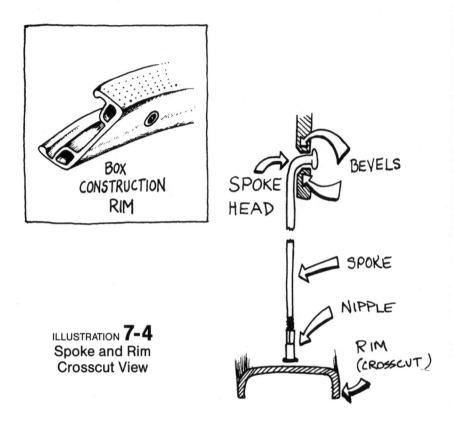

BOX CONSTRUCTION RIM

SPOKE HEAD

BEVELS

SPOKE

NIPPLE

RIM (CROSSCUT)

ILLUSTRATION **7-4**
Spoke and Rim
Crosscut View

of the spoke should be on the opposite side of the hub flange from the countersink, unless both sides of the flange are countersunk. The threaded tail end of the spoke disappears into a spoke nipple, which has flat sides and can be tightened (cl) or loosened (c-cl) with a spoke wrench [see Illustration 7-4]. Each spoke nipple fits through a hole in the *rim*. There are many different sizes and kinds of spokes, including chromed ones, "rustless" steel ones, piano wire ones, stainless steel ones, "bladed" ones, and butted ones (thicker at the ends where the stress is greater). All the spokes on any one wheel should be tightened to very nearly the same tension. If all the spokes are not the same size or kind, it is difficult to keep their tension even.

There are various sizes and kinds of rims — steel ones of various shapes, aluminum alloy ones of various shapes, and some very special tubular alloy ones which have insets in them for strength and resilience. Some rims have seams running all the way around their circumferences, others, known as "seamless" rims, are tubular or "box construction" and have only one joint where the ends of the tube meet. Seamless or tubular rims are stronger than seamed ones made of comparable materials. No matter how fancy your rim is, though, *it is fragile.* It takes very little to destroy the miraculous roundness of a bicycle wheel. Sometime when you're in a bike shop, buy a single spoke of any size. Take it in your hands and bend it. Pretty easy, isn't it? Now think of all the strain rims have to take. It can't be emphasized too much. *Spokes and rims are fragile.*

PROBLEMS: *Rim wobbles* (all bikes) I hope, after reading the above description, you won't be surprised to find, at times, that you have a wobbly wheel. Perfectly round or "true" rims are rare. Truing a wheel is a high art. Even getting a rim nearly round and evenly tightened so it will last is an art. Bending a rim takes no art or effort at all.

When your wheel wobbles, spin it, if it will spin at all. how much it wobbles by watching it at the brake shoes, or, if you have hub brakes, at a stay. If it wobbles less than ½ inch from side to side, and not at all up and down, you might have a chance of getting it tolerably straight. To locate the worst wobbles, you can put a felt tip pen against each brake shoe, so the tip is very close to the rim, then spin the wheel; marks will appear where the rim bends toward the brake on each side.

Look at the rim itself. Is the main point of wobble a little outward flare or bump in the rim — a blip, as it is called? [See Illustration 7-5.] Look at the blip. Is there a blip on both sides of the rim at the same point? Is the blip caused by the joint of a seamless or tubular rim? If your blip is small, not large enough that it misshapes the general roundness of the rim, you might have a pretty good chance of getting it out. But if you have a big blip, or more than ½ inch of side-to-side wobble, or a bad blip at the joint of the rim, or any up-and-down "hop" at all, *don't mess with that wheel.* Don't think you can fix things by tightening a spoke here or loosening one there. Take that badly blipped, wobbly, or egg-shaped wheel to a reliable shop. Ask them if they can save it. Don't hesitate to get a new rim, or even a new wheel if they suggest it. Face the music. Next time have more respect for the fragile nature of a tension-spoked wheel. If you ride a road bike, steer clear of potholes, storm drains, and curbs. If you ride a mountain bike, you can go over all those obstacles and more, but only if you have the right amount of pressure in your tires.

If your blip isn't too bad, or your wobble not too great, there is hope.

(all bikes) If you have a **blip** or a **blip and a wobble,** take care of the blip first. And remember, before you start, that you are not going to be able to make your wheel perfectly round. You are going to try to make it usable. First let the air out of the tire. For most tires, with the standard Schraeder valve, push in the little point in the valve trunk to let all the air out of the tire. You may have a Presta valve, which has a threaded point with a tiny metal cap on it that sticks out of the end of the valve trunk. [See Illustration 7-7.] To let the air out, unscrew (c-cl) the tiny cap all the way up the little threaded point until it stops, then push the threaded point in.

Get out your vise-grip (don't use any other tool) and open the jaws so that they are open wide enough to fit around the width of the rim when the handles of the vise-grip are *clamped shut.* Stick the vise-grip between the spokes of the wheel at the point where you have the blip [see Illustration 7-5]. Center the blip in the jaws of the vise-grip

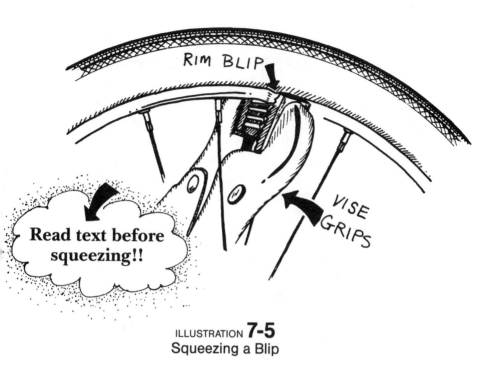

RIM BLIP

VISE GRIPS

Read text before squeezing!!

ILLUSTRATION **7-5**
Squeezing a Blip

and adjust the jaws so that they will *just barely* hold onto the blip when the handles of the tool are locked closed. Now stop. You have, at your fingertips, potential for the total destruction of the roundness of your rim. Look closely at what you are about to do. Are there blips on both sides of the rim? The vise-grip will squeeze equally from both sides. If you have a larger blip on one side than on the other, squeeze both sides of the rim until the little blip side is flat. Then take a small, thin piece of wood, like a Popsicle stick, and put it along the flattened side of the rim. Adjust the jaws of the vise-grip so that they accommodate the Popsicle stick when the handles are snapped all the way closed. Then release the little trip-lever that is on one of the vise-grip handles, and, as you keep the jaws barely gripping the rim with one hand, tighten (cl) the adjusting knob of the vise-grip so the jaws move closer to the rim. Turn the knob about ½ turn and squeeze the handles together. Watch the rim, looking at it from a tangent. If the blip is still sticking out, tighten the vise-grip adjusting knob again, ½ turn or less, and squeeze slowly. Watch as you squeeze. Stop squeezing if you're going to go too far before the vise-grip locks. *Keep in mind that you can't unsqueeze the rim!* When the blip has been squeezed in even with the rest of the rim, don't be surprised if there are two small dents, one on either side of where the blip was. They won't hurt your braking like the blip. Spin the wheel and check for a wobble. Wobble often comes along with a blip.

(all bikes) To correct a *minor wobble,* first let the air out of your tire. When trying to fix a wobble, you need to have a good reference point on at least one side of the rim. If you have hand brakes, either side-pull or center-pull, you have built-in reference points. Tighten the brakes with an adjusting sleeve if your brake system has one [see Illustrations 2-6 and 2-7]. If you have no adjusting sleeve, take a chip of wood or a trusty Popsicle stick, apply the brakes, and jam the stick between the brake hand lever and the post [see Illustrations 2-2, 2-3, and 2-4], so the brakes are on enough that the shoes just touch the rim at the wobble. If you don't have hand brakes, loosen (c-cl) one of the axle nuts of the wobbly wheel and twist the wheel so that the rim is close to a frame stay.

You want to move the section of the rim that's hitting the brake (or other reference point) away from it. For instance, to move the rim to the *left, tighten* (cl) the nipples of spokes that go to the *left* side of the hub, and *loosen* (c-cl) the nipples of the spokes that go to the *right* side of the hub. [See Illustration 7-6.]

Before you start wildly tightening and loosening spoke nipples, consider a few things. The ideal wheel has exactly the same amount of tension on every spoke. So, in your adjusting, don't leave any spoke completely loose, and don't tighten any one spoke in order to do all the rim moving. Think of a wobble as the result of a group of six or eight maladjusted spokes (not just one individualist, but a maladjusted minority — probably student spokes, whose nipples were always permissive). To move the rim laterally, you are going to want to adjust the whole group of six or eight nipples. If any of the spokes in the group you are working on are obviously much too tight or much too loose, you have to try to bring them into the same range of tightness as the other spokes in the group. You have to learn to get the "feel" of the median tension on the spokes. One way to try to get that feel is to go around the whole wheel, tightening and loosening every spoke about $\frac{1}{10}$ of a turn. You

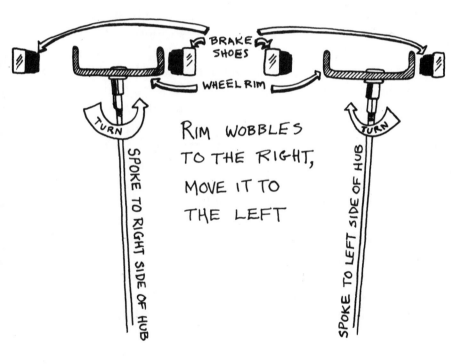

ILLUSTRATION **7-6**
Straightening a Minor Wobble

might find, right away, that all or most of the nipples are rusty, frozen to the spokes, and very difficult to turn. If your wheel has frozen nipples (a very uncomfortable condition, I'm sure), take it to a pro. *Don't mess with it.*

You will find on any rim that even in the straight sections there may be variations of tension on the spokes. This is especially true of rear wheels. The rear wheels of many bicycles are flattened or "dished" to compensate for the sprockets being on one side.

If you have a mountain bike or road bike, look straight down on the rear wheel from above. Notice that the spokes go out farther to the hub on the left side. The amount of dish necessary for most road and mountain bikes is so great that it should actually be done through the use of slightly shorter spokes on the sprocket side of the hub. Sad to say, not all rear wheels are made with shorter spokes on the right side. Dishing is sometimes done by just tightening all the spokes of the right side of the rear wheel. And for some reason it just never comes out quite as strong that way. But even on a normal front wheel, you are likely to find some spokes that are tightened up much more than others. So, as you try to take a wobble out, remember that you are not trying to make a perfect wheel. You are trying to cause a general movement of the rim without putting too much or too little tension on any one spoke.

Get the spokes in the area of your wobble into the same range of tightness as those of the rest of the wheel. One aid in doing this might be found in the spoke threads. Look closely at your spokes where they disappear into the nipples. If there are any threads showing, the number of threads should be very nearly equal on each spoke. The exception is a road or mountain bike rear wheel, where all the left side spokes should be equal and all the right side spokes shorter than the left but equal among themselves. On some of these wheels the right side spokes will be tightened more than those on the left side by about a full turn.

When the spokes are all in the same range of tightness, look again at the wobble. Loosen the spokes to the same side of the hub as the wobble and tighten the spokes to the opposite side of the hub from the wobble [see Illustration 7-6]. Adjust the whole group of six or eight spokes at the wobble, then check to see how much you've changed things. Be careful that you don't generate secondary wobbles on the ends of your original wobble. Tighten and loosen more in the middle of the wobble than at the ends. When you think you have removed the wobble, readjust the brakes, spin the wheel, and apply the brakes slowly. If the wobble isn't too bad, don't worry. The earth is slightly pear-shaped, and it has been spinning pretty well for quite a while. If your wobble is still too bad, or if the one big wobble has become several bothersome small ones, try again with a light touch and lots of patience. If your patience is running out, *quit now!* Go do something else.

When your patience is restored and you try again to get a little more roundness into your wheel, you may find that it just plays tricks on you. Wobbles appear where moments before there was only straightness. One big wobble turns into three little ones. That sort of thing. It can get like the scene in *Fantasia* with Mickey Mouse and the multiplying brooms. With a great deal of experience, you will learn that elusive feel of spoke tension that controls all these secondary wobbles. But if you are a beginner, just try to get the wheel tolerably straight. If you don't like tolerating little wobbles, take the wheel to a first-rate shop and have them true it. Make sure you patronize a first-rate shop. Many shops have people truing wheels who know very little more about it than you. A good shop will have a wheel expert who does all the wheel truing. That expert's work will cost you something, but the wheel will stay nearly straight for some time.

If the shop expert tells you that you have to replace the rim, or the whole wheel, do so if you can possibly afford to.

Just make sure you are getting equipment that's as good as the stuff you replace. In fact, if you have real fancy sealed bearing hubs, don't replace them. Save the hub and replace everything else. They last almost forever, and are so steep that it's usually much cheaper to keep your old hub and have the shop respoke it with a nice new rim.

Check for spokes sticking through a new or straightened rim before you re-inflate the tire. Put a finger under the rubber or cloth rim strip and run it all the way around the wheel. If there are spoke points sticking up more than $\frac{1}{16}$ inch, take the wheel off the bike [see *Wheel Removal*] and take the tire off the wheel with tire irons. File down those spoke ends, clean all of those sharp filings off the wheel, replace the rim strip and the tire, and put the wheel back on the bike.

Broken spokes (all bikes) This includes spokes that are stuck in their nipples and no longer adjustable, so they have to be cut. Clip them with cable clippers or wire cutters — the mashing kind are best — and treat them like other broken spokes.

If you have broken spokes, your wheel might not be worth fixing up. If the rim wobbles a little, replacing the broken spokes and truing out the wobble might be possible. But if the wobble is major and there are more than two or three broken spokes, you are going to have about a 50-50 chance of getting a nearly round wheel. Any blips or dents in the surface of the rim are going to lower your odds. If the bike has foot brakes, no brake pads grab the rim, so your wheel doesn't have to be exactly round; you can try to save it even if it's pretty bad. But if your bike has hand brakes, you want straight rims. Buy a new rim and have a good shop lace it up with new spokes. Or buy a whole new wheel; it doesn't cost much more. An old wheel with some new and some old spokes and a rusty, battered rim is not only dangerous — it is expensive if you have hand brakes that grab the rim and catch on a battered place and consequently wear the tire down in one place.

If you have a wheel with just two or three broken spokes and you think it's worth saving, take it off the bicycle [see **Wheel Removal**] and take the tire off the rim [see **Tires, removal**]. Take the broken spokes out of the hub and the rim. If you have a road or mountain bike rear wheel, chances are the broken spokes are on the side of the hub that's blocked by the cluster of sprockets on your freewheel or cassette. To get at the spoke holes on the right side of the hub, you have to remove the freewheel [see **Rear Sprocket, freewheel removal,** page 188], or take the sprockets off the cassette. Go take the sprockets off, and then come back here.

Take a good spoke off the wheel and take it, its nipple, and if it's convenient, the whole wheel to a good shop. Make sure the replacements are *exactly* the same length as your old ones, and if possible, the same thickness and made for the same kind of nipple as the old one. Get new nipples if necessary. Make sure the new spokes fit into the spoke holes of your hub.

When you stick a new spoke into its hole in the hub, make sure you stick it through so it alternates with the spokes on either side. One head in, one head out, right? Draw the new spoke through the other spokes in such a way that it will be free to reach the rim without hitting any spokes. You may have to curve the spoke a little to do this, but that's OK; it'll straighten out when it's tightened, as long as you haven't put a sharp bend in it. When you have drawn the spoke all the way in to its head, it will be pointing at the rim, but it will not be pointing at an empty spoke hole in the rim. If you are replacing several spokes, several spoke holes might look right. To find the right hole on the rim, look at the direction of the spokes on the hub. The spokes alternate, one forward, one back. You want your new spoke to go the opposite direction from the ones on either side. Move the spoke through the others until it reaches a hole in the rim. If you're still not sure that this is the right hole, check to see whether the spoke is about the right length at that hole. When you think you have the right hole, double-check by looking at the spokes that go into the rim on either side of your new one. The pattern should be the same as it is around the rest of the wheel.

When you are sure you have the new spoke aimed at the right hole, check to see if the other spokes on the wheel are laced. On almost all bikes, the spokes cross each other between the hub and the rim. On less expensive wheels, the spokes don't touch where they cross each other. On laced wheels, the spokes touch where they cross. Laced wheels are strong because any road shock coming up a spoke travels through the juncture into a second spoke, and is taken up twice as well. If your wheel is laced, make sure you weave the new spoke through the old ones in such a way that you match exactly the lacing on the rest of the wheel.

Insert a nipple through the right hole for your new, correctly laced spoke. Spin the nipple onto the spoke (cl) and tighten it with your fingers.

Repeat the procedure for any other broken spokes. Replace your sprockets (cl) if you are working on a rear wheel with a freewheel or cassette, then turn to *Tire* and *Wheel Replacement* to get your bike back in one piece. True the wheel [see *minor wobble* above], and you're all set.

TIRES

(cl) means clockwise, and usually tightens a bolt or nut.
(c-cl) means counterclockwise, and usually loosens.

DESCRIPTION AND DIAGNOSIS: (all bikes) The rubber things on the wheels that are supposed to stay full of air. There are two basic types: clinchers (sometimes called wire-ons) have separate inner tubes; sew-ups (tubulars) incorporate the tire and tube in one unit. Sew-ups are generally much lighter

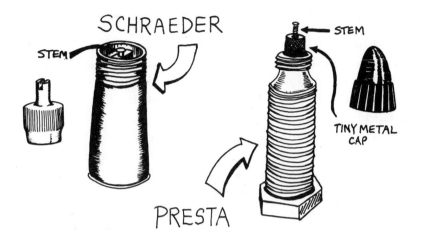

SCHRAEDER

STEM

STEM

TINY METAL
CAP

PRESTA

ILLUSTRATION **7-7**
Two Different Tire Valves

and able to take much more pressure than clinchers. But they are delicate, difficult to repair, and more expensive than clinchers. Unless you are a very serious road racer or track racer, you will probably want to use clincher tires.

All sew-up tires have Presta valves, and some clincher tires have them too. But most common clincher tire tubes now have Schraeder valves, which are similar to the tire valves on cars and are more convenient. If your clincher wheel has Presta valves and you want to switch over to the more convenient Schraeder type, just take the tire, tube, and rim strip off your wheel, then drill out the valve hole in the rim until it's just large enough to take the fatter Schraeder valve.

Clincher tires come with different treads for different surfaces. There are smooth tires for riding on smooth pavement or tracks, and there are mud tires that look like they'd work fine on tractors. Unless you do specialized racing, though, you'll probably want a tire with a smooth ridge down the middle, and some kind of tread on either side to suit your needs. If you ride a mountain bike, you might like the sound and feel of bumpy treads drumming over the pavement, but beware of riding mud-tread tires on asphalt, especially wet asphalt. Traction can be surprisingly poor.

Every tire has a recommended pressure. The tire *must* be ridden *only* with that amount of air pressure in it. Many riders, especially sew-up users, carry pressure gauges that fit over the valve stems. Riders with clincher tires can often learn to "feel" when the tire is hard enough.

There's a great **curb-edge test** you can do to make sure your tires are inflated just right. This test works no matter what kind of tire you have, no matter what kind of riding you do, and no matter how big or small you are, as long as your bike is the right size for you. To do the test, rest the wheel on the edge of a curb or stair, so the bike sticks out into the street or path, perpendicular to the curb or stair edge. Get the wheel so you can push down on it at about a 45-degree angle from above the bike. Push hard on the handlebars or seat, depending on which wheel you're testing. The curb should flare the tire out a bit but shouldn't push right through the tire and clunk against the rim. You want the tire to have a little "give" when you ride over chuckholes and rocks, in other words, but you don't want it so soft that you bottom out. If you are a hot-shot who wants tires so hard that they don't have any give, you'll have to stick to riding on clean-swept Velodrome tracks, or watch very carefully for little sharp objects on the road. Or you'll have to get used to that sudden riding-on-the-rim feeling that follows the blowout of an overblown tire. At the other extreme, if you ride a mountain bike and you want to ride with the tires really soft, for traction or that cushy feel, you should know that if the curb flares your tire all the way out and clunks on the rim when you do the pressure test, the same thing is gonna happen when you go over a big rock or chuckhole, and you may bend your rim or puncture your tire.

PROBLEMS: *Tire soft* (all bikes) Pump it up. Don't waste your precious energy riding around on soft tires. They can take the fun out of any ride, even a casual jaunt down to the corner for a beer. There are special situations when some mountain bikers like to ride with soft tires, but frankly, I'm skeptical of the value of riding on *any* tire at *any* time with so little pressure in it that it fails the curb-edge test described above. And I've been riding in the dirt for almost 40 years.

To pump up tires with Schraeder valves, screw on or push on the pump chuck (the thing that fits over the valve). Sometimes the screw-on type lets all the air out as you screw it on; if that's the case, get a new chuck with a lever for your pump. The lever type lets all the air out if you push it on too far, so push it on just far enough so it gets a good grip on the valve when you clamp the lever down. That way you'll be able to get the chuck off without letting much air out.

Make sure the tire is seated by checking the bead all the way around the tire on both sides. If there's a lump where the bead is up on the tube, let some air out of the tube, then knead and massage the side of the tire at that point, until the tube moves into the tire so the bead can settle down against the rim. Then pump until the tire feels tight to the squeeze. Release the lever and get the chuck off as fast as you can, so no air can leak out. Check the pressure by the *curb-edge test* above.

To inflate a sew-up or a fancy clincher with a Presta valve, unscrew the tiny cap on the valve, press it to make sure it's loose, then push on the chuck of the pump, making sure it goes on far enough so the rubber ring in the chuck is past the tiny cap and down on the trunk of the valve. Go easy as you push it on and also as you pump, especially with those frame-mounted hand-pumps, or you might break the valve.

Hold the part of a frame pump next to the chuck firmly with one hand as you pump with the other, and cock the thumb of the pump-holding hand against the rim of the wheel for good leverage. If you can lean the wheel against a wall or post, so the pump is braced against that solid object, you'll be even less liable to break the valve.

Pumpa, pumpa, pumpa, till sweat beads your brow. Use the **curb-edge test** above when you think you've got the tire hard. It always takes more pumpa, pumpa and cussa, cussa than you think it will.

To inflate a Schraeder valve tire or a Presta valve tire with an adapter at a gas station, *be careful!!!* Many gas stations have compressors that are made to fill truck tires up to 150 pounds per square inch or more. That kind of pressure can blow any bike tire clean away! Park or lean your bike by the pump, out of the cars' way, and so it is standing up. Spin the tire you need to fill until the valve is down at the bottom of the wheel. That way you can use the fitting on the end of the pump chuck and push down on it for a tight, accurate fit. When the chuck is on tight, squeeze the pump trigger just a *tiny* bit at a time. Little squirts of air should go in, almost like the poofs from a hand pump. Check the tire often, to make sure it isn't getting too hard. Check the bead all around on both sides of the rim, to make sure it isn't about to bulge up, allowing a huge bubble of tube to bloop out and explode in your face. When you think you've got the tire hard enough, do a careful **curb-edge test,** as above, before you ride away.

Flat tire (all bikes) Flats are due to either slow leaks, quick leaks, or blowouts. No matter what kind of flat you have, *don't ride the bike on a flat tire! Or even a soft tire!* The tire, the rim, and your life are at stake. Even pushing the bike along on a flat is bad for the tube. When you get a flat, carry the bike until you can fix it or have it fixed.

Check the valve first. Pump up the tire. Spit or put a

little water on your fingertip and place it lightly over the end of the valve. If little bubbles come through the water, see *Valve stem is loose,* page 130.

If your *clincher tire is flat,* take the wheel off the bike according to the *wheel removal* procedure. Then let all the air out of the tire (if there is any air in it) by pushing the stem top in if it's a Schraeder valve, or by unscrewing the metal cap and then pushing in the stem tip if you have a Presta valve [see Illustration 7-7].

Use your bare hands whenever you can in removing and replacing a tire. Check to see how tight the tire is on the rim by running your fingers all the way around the wheel between the tire and the rim. This will break the tire loose if it's stuck anywhere, and give you a good idea of how tough it's going to be to remove. If the tire is quite loose, grab it with both hands in one place and pull away from the center of the wheel, so that one bead (the inner edge [see Illustration 7-8]) of the tire stretches up. Lift that stretched-up place over the rim, and then work your way around the wheel, spreading the section of bead that has been pulled over the rim. This will be possible only if the tire is a loose-fitting one.

If the tire is so tight that you can't pull a section of the bead over the rim, use your tire irons. Do *not* use a screwdriver or any other substitute. Stick the round end of the tire iron a little way under one of the beads of the tire. Make sure you aren't getting both beads of the tire, with the tube pinched in between. Pinching the tube can easily put a hole in it, even if you are using tire irons. When you have the iron under one bead of the tire, pry the iron all the way out and down and hook the handle end of it on a spoke [see Illustration 7-8]. With a second iron, pry out more of the bead a couple of inches from your first pry. If you need to make a third pry, do it about 3 inches farther down the line, but usually two pries will get the tire bead well on its

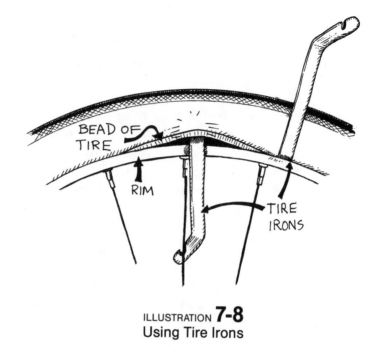

ILLUSTRATION **7-8**
Using Tire Irons

way. When the tire bead is on its way, in other words, when it doesn't try to jump back onto the rim, take all the tire irons out, stick one iron between the popped-out bead and the rim, and peel the rest of the bead out of the rim. You've now got the tire half off the rim, and you shouldn't take it any farther off.

Pull the tube out of the tire on the side that has the bead out of the rim, *except* where it is held by the valve. Leave the valve in the rim and most of the tube out of the rim and out of the tire. Pump up the tube until it swells to about 1½ times its normal size. If you can't pump up the tube, the leak is pretty big and the tube should be replaced. If the tube fills up, look for the leak. When you find it, mark it on the tube. Use either a big bull's-eye circle mark, or a "cross hair" mark with the hole in the middle. Push the tube back next to the tire and look at the tire and rim of the wheel where the puncture is. Look for tacks or pieces of glass or sharp pieces of metal stuck in the tire, or a sharp burr in the rim, or a sharp spoke tail sticking through the rim strip. When you have found and removed or filed down the cause of your tube leak, you can completely deflate the tube. To get the valve out of the hole in the rim, first unscrew the cap and sleeve around the valve if you have either, then pull a section of *the bead that you have already removed* back over to the opposite side of the tube at the valve. Now you can slip the valve out of the hole in the rim by pulling on the tube.

If you have a small hole in your tube, you can patch it. If you have two tiny holes next to each other ("snake bites" caused by riding over bumps on under-inflated tires) you can patch both holes, sometimes with one patch. But if the hole is much larger than a pin-prick, or if the leak is at the base of the valve, replace the tube. Many shops replace any tube with a leak. They quote Webster, who states that a patch is a "temporary repair." They say that their shops do only permanent repairs. They have a good point. You can get fairly inexpensive tubes. But if you have a small puncture in your tube, and you don't mind the idea of temporary repairs (what isn't temporary, you might ask in response to Webster), get a bicycle tube patching kit and follow its instructions. Different kits have different methods, but the general procedure is simple.

Clean and dry the tube, then scrape it with an abrasive, like the scraper on the lid of the patch kit, or a piece of sandpaper. Get your fingers as clean and dry as possible, then spread a thin, even film of glue all around the hole, making sure that the area you cover is bigger than the patch you're going to use. Wipe off any thick globs, or they won't dry and seal up tight.

When the whole area of glue turns from shiny to that dull-surface color that means it's dry (it only takes five minutes or so), peel the tinfoil backing off the patch (leave the cellophane on there) and stick the patch in place, without touching the glue or the sticky side of the patch. Pinch and knead the patched tube between your fingers, starting at the center of the patch and working out to the edges. Squeeze it as hard as your fingers can. I like to stack up my thumbs and index fingers of both hands, for a double squeeze. When the patch is stuck on there, take a little fine dust or talcum powder or something, and poof it around the patch, so the extra glue on the tube won't stick to the inside of the tire or wheel. Replace the tube and tire and it will be ready for immediate use.

If you decide to replace your leaky tube with a new inexpensive one, you should check the valve stem of your new tube. Pump up the tube until it is 1½ times its normal size, then spit or put a little water on your fingertip and put your fingertip loosely over the end of the valve.

If little bubbles come out between your fingertip and the valve, the *valve stem is loose.* To tighten it, you need either a fancy stem tool that you can buy at a bike shop, or one of the metal valve caps that have two prongs on top of them [see Illustration 7-9]. A bike shop might give you one of those, or sell it to you for very little. When you have a valve tool or metal valve cap with the prongs, stick the prongs down the valve trunk and turn them back and forth until you feel them slip over the little arms of the stem. Now tighten (cl) the stem. Not too hard, especially if you

ILLUSTRATION **7-9**
Two-Pronged
Metal Cap

have the fancy tool. Those stems are delicate. Try the wet finger test again. If there are bubbles, you might have a lemon of a tube. The store might replace the valve stem, or the whole tube, if you're lucky.

To replace the clincher tube, and tire, start by letting almost all the air out of the tube. If you are putting in a new tube, put just a little bit of air in it so it isn't flat and unworkable. If you are putting on a new tire, get one of the beads around the rim, using your bare hands *only*. If you can't get the tire bead on, it's the wrong size. It might be hard to get the last inches of the bead over the rim, but puff and cuss and get it on by hand.

If it's all too easy to get that first bead on, and you're mounting a new mountain bike tire on a fancy lightweight box-construction rim, do a quick check to make sure you don't have an oversize tire that may pop off your fancy rim. Put both beads on the fancy rim, without a tube inside. Then pull one side of the tire away from the rim, and see if you can stick your index finger through the gap between the edge of the rim and the two tire beads. If you can, the tire is too big for that special rim. Don't take a chance on blowing it off the wheel or rolling it off in a sharp turn at high speed. Find a tire that fits more snugly. Then mount just one bead of it.

When you have one tire bead in the rim and one bead off the edge of the rim, check the rim strip; make sure it is a thin rubber one, and make sure it is stretched flat around the whole rim. Then get the tire bead down in the "groove" of the rim with the rim strip. Push the tire from the side that has the bead off the rim over to the opposite side of the hole in the rim for the tube valve. Push the valve in and now pop that section of the tire back over the tube. Working away from the valve in both directions, stuffing the tube up into the tire and over onto the rim. Make sure the tube doesn't get twisted in the process.

Then work the remaining tire bead over the lip of the rim with your thumbs, making sure the tube doesn't get pinched between the tire bead and the rim. When you get down to the last few inches of the tire bead, it will get tough. Roll up your sleeves. Make sure the tube is tucked up onto the rim where it won't get pinched, and make sure that almost all the air is out of the tube. Work with both thumbs on one part of the remaining bead at a time; don't try to pop the whole thing over at once until you have only about 3 or 4 inches left. At this point you can hold one part of the bead in place, like the right hand is doing in the illustration, and roll the rest of the bead into place with the palm or heel of your left hand. Don't slam the wheel around in your excitement — wheels bend easily. And *don't* use a screwdriver, or, if you can possibly avoid it, even a tire iron. Anything that you stick under the tire at this juncture could reach inside the rim, grab the tube, and pinch it. So use your hands and your patience and your perseverance. Franz Kafka once said, "There is only one human sin — impatience." Not that I expect you to keep your patience when that tire bead bites your finger, then jumps off the rim. When you've just got to throw something, don't throw the wheel. Grab a handy box wrench and throw it. It will make a much more satisfying clang, and it won't bend. Just be careful where you throw it.

When you get the tire over the rim, first push the valve in and out of the rim a couple of times to make sure the tube isn't pinched between the tire bead and the rim right next to the valve. Then go have a beer or indulge in whatever relaxes you. When you are restored, come back and pump up the tire. If it goes flat, do the wet finger test on the valve. If the valve is OK, it must be the tube. Call the tire and tube what they are, and start all over. I know exactly how you feel. If the tire holds air, replace the wheel [see **Wheel Replacement**], then celebrate with another relaxer and a restorer, too. It *is* a marvel when all that air pressure actually stays inside that skinny little tube, isn't it?

If you have lotsa trouble keeping the air in your tires, if you get lotsa flats, in other words, here are some preventive measures that may help. Use as wide a cross-section tire as you can on your rear wheel (some 1-inch rims will take a 1⅛-inch tire, some 1¼-inch rims will accept a 1⅜-inch tire) and pump the thing up to the maximum allowed pressure when you're going to be riding over rough terrain. Watch out for patches of glittering glass along the road as you ride, and skirt around these hazards. Don't ride up and down curbs. Go on a spare-tire reducing diet, i.e., ride more, eat less; the less you weigh, the less of a spare tire you'll have around your middle, and the less you'll be using spare tires due to flats.

(Rd bike) If you have a *flat sew-up or tubular tire,* let me put my cards on the table. I think sew-ups are for racing or very, very specialized road riding. I don't use sew-ups on my own bikes. Sew-ups cost more and are more vulnerable, so if you can afford that kind of luxury, I recommend you have a pro fix your flat sew-ups. Or if you want to master the art, most sew-up patch kits have adequate instructions.

Whether you take your sew-ups to a shop or patch them yourself, you'll want to be able to take them off the rim and put them back. *To remove a sew-up from the rim,* push it with your fingers off one side of the rim, being careful to keep the glued-on rim strip stuck to the tire. When the tire is all removed except the valve stem, pull the stem straight out of its hole in the rim.

To mount a sew-up on the rim, completely deflate the tire and stretch it gently. Make a figure 8 out of it and hook one loop under a crooked knee. Stick an arm through the other loop and slip it over your shoulder. Stretch it gently, until you hear a tiny crickly-crackly noise of the casing expanding, then *stop* stretching. Take it off before it breaks or twaps you. Spread an even film of rim cement around the rim and let it dry until it is tacky. Put the tire valve in its hole, and work around the rim away from the valve with both hands, pushing the tire onto the rim with your thumbs in such a way that the tire goes on evenly and you don't get glue on yourself, the tire, or the outside of the rim. That's a trick. Work slowly. Put on the section of the tire that's opposite the valve last, trying to keep the tension even all the way around, so the valve isn't pulled one way or the other. When the tire is on, pump it up partially so it assumes its normal shape. Then go around the wheel, lifting, moving, and reseating the portions of the tire that are to one side or the other. Spin the wheel to check for trueness of the tire. Trueness is very important, because any tire wobble will cause excessive wear. When you are satisfied with the trueness of the tire, pump it up so it's good and hard, and leave it for at least half a day to let the glue dry before you ride on it. Riding on a sew-up that has wet glue can make for a very oddly shaped tire. While you're waiting for the glue to dry, it might be a good idea to wipe off that unavoidable extra that somehow gets on the outside of the rim, or the tire, or you. Fancy bike shops sell a solvent made just for the purpose. Don't use any other solvent; you might ruin the tires or the braking surface of the rim.

To keep sew-up flats to a minimum, you can graze the palm of a gloved hand over the surface of the tire after you ride through a patch of glass or sharp-looking rubbish. Most

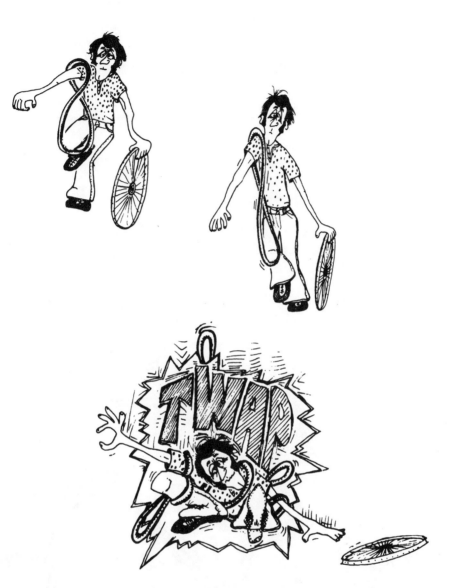

punctures in tires are caused not when a sharp object is first hit, but when it works its way through the rubber and cloth casing into the tube after many successive revolutions of the wheel. You can often "rub out" little sharp things before they work their way through the tire and tube. Don't do this with bare hands, though. To help avoid unexpected blow-outs, let a little pressure out of each tire after you finish a ride. But don't forget to pump up before the next ride.

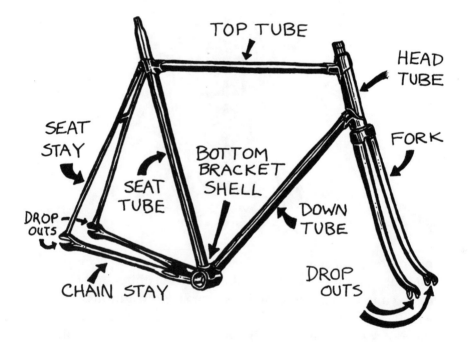

TOP TUBE

HEAD TUBE

SEAT STAY

BOTTOM BRACKET SHELL

SEAT TUBE

FORK

DROP OUTS

DOWN TUBE

CHAIN STAY

DROP OUTS

ILLUSTRATION **8-1**
Frame

8
Frame

(cl) means clockwise, and usually tightens a bolt or nut.
(c-cl) means counterclockwise, and usually loosens.

DESCRIPTION: (all bikes) The frame consists of a horizontal (or nearly horizontal) top tube, a head tube at the front of the bike, a seat tube parallel (or nearly parallel) to the head tube, a diagonal down tube from the head to the bottom bracket, chain stays from the bottom bracket to the rear drop-outs, and seat stays from the rear drop-outs to the top of the seat tube [see Illustration 8-1].

The frame is more than it might seem. It is not just a lopsided diamond and two triangles of tubing brazed or welded or bonded together. It is the heart and soul of a bicycle. It is not just the most expensive part of the bike. It is the single most significant part in determining the quality of a bike. The frame is also the single most difficult part to repair. When you are looking at a bike you want to buy, look at the frame first. Is it made of good tubing? Columbus, Tange, and Ishiwata double-butted are among the best.

Double-butted tubing is thin and springy and light in the middle, and thicker and stronger at the ends, where the stress is. There are too many other good types of tubing for everyday bikes to list here. There are also high-quality aluminum frames, and frames made out of high-tech resin/ fiber materials. Then there are the frames made of cheapo steel tubing that is very heavy and really should have been left to do the plumbing.

To distinguish good from bad tubing, first pick up the bike. If it weighs a ton, that usually means that its tubes are thick to make up for their weakness. If the bike is light, put it upright on a flat surface and stand to one side of it. Make sure the tires are inflated to the proper pressure. Grab the handlebar nearest you with one hand, and the seat with the other. Hold the bike firmly and tilt it away from you. Put one foot *gently* on the end of the bottom bracket axle. Give a *light* push with your toe. Go easy; one quick way to alienate a bike dealer is to start kicking and shoving new bikes around. When you push lightly with your toe, the frame should flex slightly, then spring back. If you want to educate your toe to the right feel, try the bottom bracket push test on a super-expensive road racing machine. Tiny bit of give, quick spring-back. Feel it? Try the same test on a 50-pound balloon-tire cruiser. Some difference, isn't there? The cruiser either doesn't give at all or gives and then is sluggish in coming back to straight. (Which isn't to say that cruisers are useless. I have one for beach riding.) This test doesn't take into account the difference in tire size and hardness. Comparing a mountain bike with soft tires to a road-racing machine with rock-hard tires will not give fair results, for instance. But if you compare similar models, and all of them have the tires inflated properly, you can get a fair idea of the frames' springiness.

The best test for any frame, of course, is riding the bike. But it's hard to tell how good a bike is on the first ride. If you are an experienced rider, you can trust your "feel" after one ride on a new bike. If you are new to the game, take this into account.

Different bikes have different types of joints. Mountain bikes will often have TIG (Tungsten Inert Gas) welded joints. [See Illustration 8-2.] These joints don't look real pretty, but extensive testing in the best labs (steep, rocky,

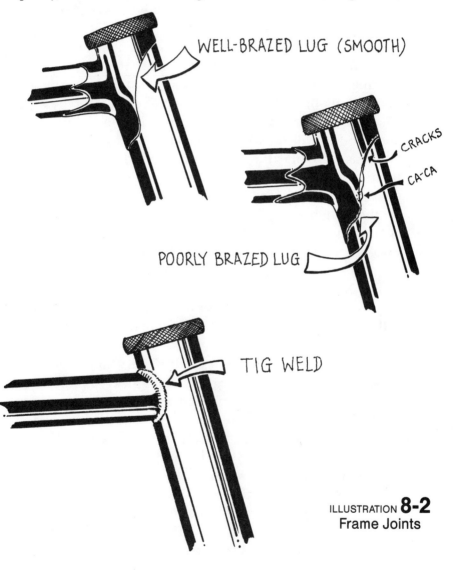

WELL-BRAZED LUG (SMOOTH)

CRACKS

CA-CA

POORLY BRAZED LUG

TIG WELD

ILLUSTRATION **8-2**
Frame Joints

muddy mountain bike race courses) has proven that TIG-welded bike frames can hold up under the worst punishment, even if they are made out of relatively light tubes. Any reputable TIG-welded frame will be reliable.

Many road bikes and some mountain bikes have brazed joints. These vary in quality more than TIG-welded joints. The tubes are usually brazed into little metal sleeve joints called lugs [see Illustration 8-2]. On some bikes the tubes are cut to fit and "fillet" brazed. Brazing is done at relatively low temperatures, to avoid making the frame tubing brittle. Brazing is a high art. If you look closely at the edges of any lug on a lug-brazed bike, you can see the marks of the artist who did the brazing. If he was great, the joint of the tube and the lug will be perfectly smooth all the way around. Obvious globs of extra around the edges of the lug, or little holidays where you can see a crack back under the lug are the signs of a mediocre frame builder. For more information on the design and construction of frames, read the *Frame* chapter in *Bike Tripping;* the chapter is by Al Eisentraut, who is a great master of the art. I'm not saying you must buy a frame that's made by a great frame builder. I'm just saying that if you get a not-so-great brazed frame, you have to be kind to it. Any bike, even one with fat welded joints, will last if you respect it for what it is — good, reliable transportation.

Frame problems, such as a broken joint, a bent or broken tube, or a loss of alignment, are next to impossible to repair. I don't recommend that you try doing it or even having it done, unless you have access to a highly trained bicycle frame builder. Don't ever try to weld a broken or cracked frame tube. If your frame bends or breaks, you usually have to get a new frame. So when you buy a bike, buy one with a frame that will do the job you want it to. Then don't expect more of it than you should.

One note about *paint:* new frames usually have good paint jobs. Keep the original paint on a frame as long as possible. Keep the bike out of the rain and touch up scratches with auto touch-up paint to prevent rust. To re-paint a frame you have to take everything off it. If you're up to that, use the various sections of this book that apply. If not, have a good shop do the job. Do-it-yourself painting means first thoroughly strip the old paint (use a liquid paint remover). The frame has to be perfectly clean and dry. Then spray on a coat or two of primer, making each coat as smooth as possible and always letting it dry thoroughly before spraying the next coat. Then several layers of spray-on epoxy paint. Or you can take the bare frame to an auto paint shop and get a bake-on job. You might get it done pretty cheaply if you're willing to have them put the frame through the works with an auto body. Just wait for one that has a color you like.

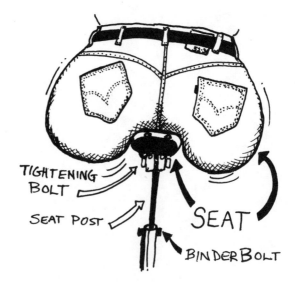

ILLUSTRATION **9-1**
The Seat

9
Seat

(cl) means clockwise, and usually tightens a bolt or nut.
(c-cl) means counterclockwise, and usually loosens.

DESCRIPTION: (all bikes) The seat is the leather or plastic thing you sit on. It is attached by a heavy wire frame and a bracket or clamp to a seat post. The post is held by a pinned binderbolt in the seat tube of the bike frame [see Illustration 9-1], or it is clamped there by a quick release lever. Sizes, shapes, hardnesses, and durabilities of different seats vary widely. If you plan to ride long distances, you should get a quality nylon, leather-covered nylon, or top-grade butt leather seat. You can get a comfortable seat if you shop around. The ones with carefully placed soft spots of gel are especially good for people with tender points.

Seat brackets, which fit on the top end of plain seat posts, are standardized at ⅞ inch. The kind of seat post that has a clamp built onto the top has standardized slots for the seat frame rails [see Illustration 9-2]. But the o.d.'s (outside diameters) of seat posts where they fit into the seat tube of the

143

bike frame are anything but standardized. They vary from about ⅞ inch to 1⅛ inch. Often they are calibrated on a metric scale.

The clamp-top seat posts are often adjustable to a much finer degree than the standard seat brackets. If you have one of these fancy units, all you need is the right size allen wrench to adjust the seat's position. And once you adjust the seat and tighten it into place, it will stay put. Bracket seat mounts aren't so reliable; they tend to strip out and come loose.

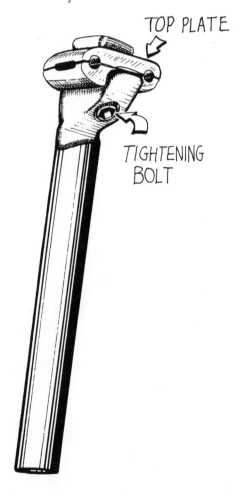

TOP PLATE

TIGHTENING BOLT

ILLUSTRATION **9-2**
Clamp-Top Seat Post

A note for those of you who have mountain bikes with quick-release binderbolts holding your seat post in the frame: thieves tend to steal seats that are held in by quick-release binderbolts. A most inconvenient drawback to this convenience item. One solution is to get a special custom binderbolt that works just like a quick-release, but does not have a lever. Instead, it has a hole in the end for an allen wrench. You just stick the allen wrench in there and use it like a lever. Unless a bike thief has this allen wrench (most casual bike thieves won't) your seat is secure.

PROBLEMS: *Seat loose* (all bikes) If it tilts forward and back on the end of the post, and you have a bracket holding the seat, get a box end, open end, or crescent wrench that fits the tightening nuts exactly, and tighten them up (cl—see Illustration 9-1). Tighten them evenly, doing a few turns on one, then a few on the other, and as you tighten, shift the seat slightly every once in a while to make sure that the bracket is sitting firmly in the position you want. If you have lots of trouble with your seat bracket coming loose, I recommend you buy a new seat post, the kind with the clamp built onto the end.

If you have a tilty seat held by a clamp on top of the seat post, loosen (c-cl) the allen screw or screws with the right size allen wrench, then jiggle and shift the seat around until you have it where you want it, then tighten up (cl) the allen screw(s) thoroughly. [See Illustration 9-2.] If it doesn't stay put, the top plate of the clamp may be stripped. Take the allen screw(s) all the way out (c-cl) and replace the top plate, then adjust the seat and tighten (cl) the screws thoroughly.

I'm not going to tell you what seat position is right for you. You might be built differently from me. Generally, it's been my experience that many people, especially women, like their seats tipped forward slightly from level. I happen to like mine tipped back ever so slightly. But the seat should be close to level. If it isn't, either your weight will be thrown forward too much, or your crotch will get very sore.

(all bikes) If your *seat swivels from side to side,* or if the whole post slides down into the frame tube, set the post at the right height for you. I'm not going to tell you what your right height is. Generally, though, people like the seat set at such a level that when they sit on it, they can put the pedal at the bottom of its stroke, stretch their leg out straight, and rest their heel flat on the pedal. Measure pedal length with *your* seat centered on the bike seat so that as you pedal down the road *your* seat doesn't have to rock from side to side on the bike seat, which creates a particularly distressing friction. Then check to make sure the seat isn't so low that your knees fold way up at the top of each pedal stroke and hit you in the chest. When you get the seat where you want it, tighten (cl) the binderbolt or quick-release lever [see Illustration 9-1]. If you have an allen bolt for a binderbolt, get the correct size allen wrench and tighten (cl) the bolt thoroughly. If you have a binderbolt with a hex nut on it, use a box end wrench if you can get one or an open end wrench that fits well, or a carefully used crescent wrench.

If you have a quick-release lever and tightening it doesn't hold the seat tight, release the lever and turn the nut on the other end of the binderbolt by hand, clockwise, about ¼ turn or less. Don't overtighten it, or you'll mash and misshape the frame and possibly the seat post when you squeeze too hard on it. If you have a mountain bike with one of those custom quick-release binderbolts that has an allen wrench hole instead of a lever, just get the correct size allen wrench, stick it in, and use it like a lever (don't turn the wrench too much; keep in mind that it's a lever, not a wrench now).

You standard binderbolt people really have to tighten (cl) that binderbolt pretty well. If you don't have a wrench that fits it, you can bugger the bolt easily. So be firm, but careful. The best approach is to loosen (c-cl) the nut a bunch, put a drop of oil on the bolt threads, then tighten (cl) the nut smoothly and thoroughly. If the bolt spins as you turn on the nut, it probably has a stripped pin. Take the nut off, using the vise-grip to hold the bolt if necessary, and take the bolt out. Replace it with an exact duplicate. If the hole in the frame for the pin on the bolt is ruined, you have to resort to a bolt with a hex head that you can hold with a wrench as you tighten (cl) the nut up.

If no amount of tightening on the binderbolt will tighten up the frame tube on the seat post, you have a post that's too small for your frame tube. Get a post that's the right size, or get a shim — a thin, curved piece of metal — and put it around the post where the binderbolt will clamp on it. Then tighten up (cl) on the binderbolt.

If, by some chance, you have a post that is too big for your frame tube, don't force it into the tube. It will stretch and weaken the frame at that point. Get a post that fits, or get one that's too small and shim it.

Seat saggy (all bikes) You have an old leather seat. When you sit on it, you sink down until your bottom rests on all the wrong places. You want to get the seat tight enough that you rest on the correct place. To stretch the seat tighter, use an open end wrench to tighten (cl) the nut that's on a long bolt under the front end of the seat. If the whole bolt spins, you have to grip it with the vise-grip at the back end of the bolt, or with a pair of pliers at the front end, or with a little open end wrench if the back end of the bolt is squared off. It might be easier if you loosen (c-cl) the tightening nuts on the bracket and take the seat off the bike. Getting an open end wrench around the nut on the long bolt and turning it is a trick. You often have to push the leather back and forth to get the wrench in and out. But have patience and persevere. Or just buy one of those neato gel-padded seats that suits your tush, and enjoy.

10
Power Train

(cl) means clockwise, and usually tightens a bolt or nut.
(c-cl) means counterclockwise, and usually loosens.

DESCRIPTION AND DIAGNOSIS: (all bikes) If the frame of a bicycle is its heart and soul, the power train is the bike's blood and guts. The power train delivers some percentage of the energy that you put into the pedals to the back wheel of your bike. The front half on a 1-speed or 3-speed cruiser consists of the pedals, the cranks, the bottom bracket set, and the front sprocket or chainwheel. On a mountain bike or road bike there will be two or three front sprockets and a front changer to move the chain from sprocket to sprocket. The back half on a 1-speed bike consists of a rear sprocket. A 3-speed bike has a 3-speed hub, and mountain and road bikes have rear sprockets or cogs (anywhere from five to eight of them), and a derailleur-type changer. On all bikes, a chain connects the front and back halves. The better all of these parts work, the more efficient your system is, and the more of your energy will get to the rear wheel.

(all bikes) If there are nasty **grinding, rubbing, squeaking, kerchunking, or clunking noises** when you pedal, you can make an easy test to find out if you have a power train problem. Get going at a good clip on a quiet, level place or a slight downhill grade, then just coast. If the nasty noises do not stop when you stop pedaling, your problem is in the back wheel, not the power train. See **Hub Problems** (page 104) and check for **brake stickies** under **Brakes** (page 30).

If a nasty noise appears only when you pedal, see if it repeats itself. If it repeats itself each time your pedal makes a revolution, then it's probably a **Front Half Problem** (see below). If it repeats itself once for approximately each two revolutions of your pedal, then you have a chain problem; go directly to **Chain Problems** (page 172). If the noise repeats itself two to three times for every revolution of the pedal, then you probably have a back-half problem; see **Rear Changer Problems** (page 213) and **Rear Sprocket Problems** (page 186). If the noise is constant, unvarying, you have to find out where it is by listening and watching all the parts of the power train. It's easier and safer to do this sort of observation with the bike up on a rack or floor stand [see Tools]. When you think you know which part of the power train is acting up, turn to that section.

If you have multiple gears, a constant noise or problem might be due to a faulty gear changer system. Each of the two types of system, derailleur and hub, is treated as a whole for basic adjustments and maintenance.

Derailleur gear people: If the chain comes off the sprockets, either the front ones or the back ones, or if you can't get the chain to go onto any of the sprockets, see the **Derailleur Systems: General** section (page 192); check **Chain Problems** (page 172), too. If you hear a plunk-plunking noise when you're in low gear and the chain is on the largest of the rear sprockets, STOP RIDING!!! That innocuous little sound is a warning that the rear changer (derailleur) is out

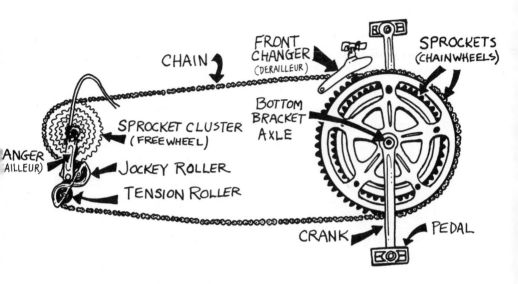

of adjustment, and just about to self-destruct in the spokes.
See *Derailleur Systems: General* to save the derailleur by
adjusting it (page 192).

　(Cruisers) Three-speed people: If your *gears slip* or
change by themselves, or you can't get into a gear (usually
second), or the gear level gets stuck, or you can't get out of a
gear at all (usually high), see *Hub Changer,* at the end of this
chapter.

Front Half: General

DESCRIPTION AND DIAGNOSIS: (all bikes) The front half of
the power train consists of the pedals, the cranks, the bottom
bracket set, the front sprocket(s) or chainwheel(s), and, if you
have a mountain or road bike, a front changer [see Illustration 10-1]. The front changer is not included in this section,
however, but is under *Gear Changers: General* (page 191).

If you have a front half problem, you have to find out where it is, and then go to the section on that unit. If you have a derailleur gear system and your *chain is throwing,* or your *gear is slipping,* or your *changer is rubbing* on the chain all the time, see *Gear Changers: General* (page 191). If your *chain goes kerchunk* and jumps each time it hits a certain point of the front sprocket, see *Front Sprocket Problems* (page 181). If you hear nasty noises at each revolution of the pedal, first check the pedal itself [see Illustrations 10-2 and 10-3]. Is it hard to revolve on its spindle by hand? Is it loose on the spindle? Is it obviously bent? When you spin it by hand, does it catch and grab? Have the dust cap and/or the locknut come off? For any of these symptoms, see *Pedal Problems,* below.

If you hear a *clunk* or sharp *squeak* each time you push down on one pedal or the other, or if you sometimes feel a slight *slipping of a pedal* as you push hard on it, or if *one of your cranks is knocking* on the frame or your kick stand each time it comes around, see *Crank Problems* (page 158).

If you hear grinding noises that you can't pin down on the pedals, or if your whole front half can slip back and forth or wiggle in the frame, or if the whole front half is hard to turn, then see *Bottom Bracket* (page 164).

PEDALS

(cl) means clockwise, and usually tightens a bolt or nut.
(c-cl) means counterclockwise, and usually loosens.

DESCRIPTION: (all bikes) What you push on with your feet to make the bike go. A pedal consists of a metal, plastic, or metal and rubber platform, a spindle which is screwed into the crank, and bearing sets on which the platform revolves around the spindle. There is often a dust cap screwed or wedged onto the end of the spindle over the bearings. [See Illustration 10-3.] There are also sealed-bearing pedals. Mountain bikes often have a large, metal platform that you

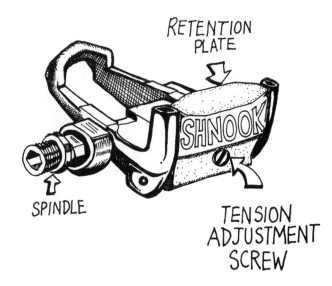

RETENTION
PLATE

SPINDLE

SHNOOK

TENSION
ADJUSTMENT
SCREW

ILLUSTRATION **10-2**
Clipless Pedal

can replace if it gets bent or broken. Road bikes often have clipless pedals, which require special cleats on your cycling shoes.

PROBLEMS: *Pedal loose or tight and noisy* (Mt bike, Cruiser) First make sure the spindle is screwed tightly into the crank. Tighten it if it isn't. Use a strong, flat, open-ended wrench on the flats you can see on the spindle between the crank and the pedal platform. If you can't find a standard wrench that fits in there, buy a special pedal spanner from a shop or catalog. The right pedal tightens *clockwise;* the left pedal tightens *counterclockwise.* [See Illustration 10-4.]

Pedal still acting up? You have to **adjust the bearings.** If you have a dust cap over the outer end of the spindle, see if the cap has flat sides that you can put a big wrench or channel lock on. If there is some sort of wrenchable surface, unscrew (c-cl) the dust cap. If there are no wrenchable surfaces, pry the dust cap off with a thin-bladed screwdriver.

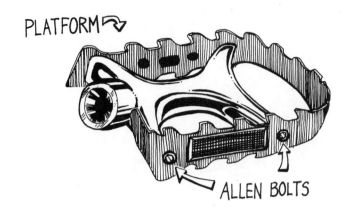

PLATFORM

ALLEN BOLTS

CONE   DUST CAP

SPINDLE   BEARINGS   LOCKNUT

ILLUSTRATION **10-3**
Pedal, Exploded View

Look inside. If you can wiggle the pedal back and forth on the spindle, back off (c-cl) the locknut on the end of the spindle, tighten (cl) the cone behind the locknut and back it off ¼ turn (c-cl), then tighten (cl) the locknut. Put a drop of oil in there and try to get a drop into the bearings at the other end of the pedal too. If the pedal is tight (hard to turn), adjust the cone to make it looser (c-cl). As with all bearings, make the adjustment tight enough that there is no wiggle, but loose enough that the bearings turn freely without binding.

If you don't have a locknut and cone set-up under the dust cap, the pedal doesn't have ball bearings, and you can't adjust it. It may be a fancy pedal with sealed cartridge bearings, or it may be a cheap pedal with no ball bearings at all. If you can possibly afford to, replace cheapo pedals with ball bearing ones.

If adjusting the pedal bearings doesn't solve the problem, you can do a *pedal overhaul,* even though a pedal is never the same after it has made grinding and scraping noises. Put the pedal over a clean white rag. Take the dust cap off, if you haven't already, with a channel lock (or a screwdriver if it's the wedged-on kind). Back (c-cl) the locknut all the way off the spindle, and take the washer off. Hold the pedal on the spindle with one hand, and back (c-cl) the cone off the bearings. Count the bearings as they come. When they are all out of that end of the pedal, take the whole pedal platform off the spindle and count and catch the remaining bearings as they come. Clean all parts and replace any that are scored or dented. Are the bearing races in the platform scored? If they aren't, you can put grease in them and reconstruct the pedal. Adjust your reconstructed pedal as described in the *pedal loose* section above. If the bearing surfaces in the pedal are scored, you might as well get a new pedal, as described in the next problem.

Pedal bent, broken, or stripped off (Mt bike, Cruiser) On some mountain bike pedals, like the one in the illustration, there are little allen bolts that hold the platform of the pedal to the frame of it. You can just unscrew (c-cl) those little bolts and put on a new platform if your old one is beat to shreds. But if you have a beat-up pedal that doesn't have a replaceable platform, replace the whole pedal *now!* A spindle, or a weak, bent-up pedal is a dangerous thing. Make sure you get a pedal that fits your crank. The best way to match a pedal is to take the bike and a wrench that fits it to the bike store. Get an open end wrench that fits snugly on the flat places on the pedal spindle, in between the pedal and the crank. A crescent wrench won't fit in that space; a $\frac{9}{16}$-inch or 15-mm open end wrench is what you need in most cases.

When you get to the shop with your bike and wrench, take the old pedal off. Remember, the right pedal loosens c-cl, left pedal loosens cl. You may have to borrow or buy a special pedal spanner to loosen your pedal if it is really tight or rusted into place. If possible, get the wrench or spanner and crank in the "closing V" formation shown in Illustration 10-4, so you can get maximum leverage.

Get an *exact* replacement for your pedal, checking it right there to make sure it fits in your crank. If the threads on the new pedal fit real tight or real loose in your crank

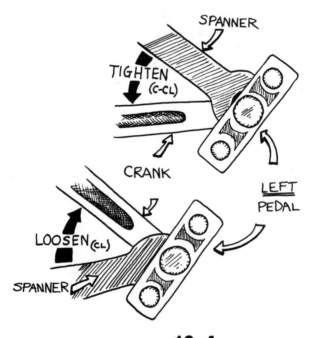

ILLUSTRATION **10-4**
Left Pedal: Left-Hand Threads

(especially if the crank is aluminum), *don't* force the pedal on or try to tighten it in spite of its loose fit. The threads may be from different countries, and therefore cut at different angles; get a pedal with threads that match right, no matter how much of a hassle it is.

Clipless pedal retention plate loose (Rd bike) Your shoe slips around in the retention plate of your clipless pedal. First check to make sure the screws holding the cleat to your shoe are tight (cl). Adjust the position of the cleat so your heel just misses the crank as it spins by, then tighten (cl) the cleat screws thoroughly. If your shoe has a very sharply curved sole so the cleat can't fit flat against it, put a little shim (flat piece of metal) or a dime under the front end before you tighten the screw down. If the cleat is worn down from walking on it, mark the place where the cleat is on your shoe (trace around it with a pen), then take the screws out. Notice which length screws go in which holes, and put them back in the same holes. Get a new cleat just like the old one. When mounting it, make sure the screws go into the same holes they came out of.

Usually fixing up the cleat will take care of your loose clipless pedal. If not, you have to **adjust or replace the retention plate.** To adjust the spring tension on it, turn the adjusting screw in (cl). GO EASY! Whether you have a big screw like the one shown in Illustration 10-2, or a screw with an allen head, or a little adjusting screw on the top surface of the pedal, you have to turn that screw carefully, to avoid stripping the threads. Don't turn it too far in either direction. On the big-screw type, you have about 2½ turns from minimum tension to all the way tight. The little-screw type only allows about a single turn from minimum to maximum tension. So don't expect to make unlimited changes to the spring tension with that screw. The safest way to do an adjustment on either kind is to turn the screw in (cl) all the way, GENTLY, without forcing it when it reaches the end of its range. Then try the tension and loosen (c-cl) the screw a bit at a time if you need to. Make sure you do not loosen the big-screw type more than 2½ turns. And when you finish adjusting the tension on one pedal, adjust the other one to get them equal.

If you have the big-screw type of retention plate and the plate is real loose or cracked or worn down, you can replace the whole plate by loosening (c-cl) the big screw all the way. Get a kit for your kind of pedal at a bike shop, then put the new plate on carefully, screwing the adjusting screw in until it stops, then backing it off 2½ turns or less. If you have the little-screw type of retention plate and it gets too loose or beat up, you have to take the pedal off and let a shop that carries those pedals do the replacement.

CRANKS

(cl) means clockwise, and usually tightens a bolt or nut.
(c-cl) means counterclockwise, and usually loosens.

DESCRIPTION: (all bikes) The cranks are the sturdy bars of solid metal that attach your pedals to the axle of the bottom bracket. The pedal is screwed into the crank. The crank is usually held to the bottom bracket axle by a bolt that goes through the crank and into the end of the axle, or by a nut on a threaded stud that sticks out from the end of the axle. On some American cruisers, the two cranks and the bottom bracket axle are one solid piece of steel. On some European bikes, the cranks are held to the axle by a wedge-shaped cotter pin. The cranks, in order of mention, are called cotterless cranks, Ashtabula (such a beautiful name!) cranks, and cottered cranks. [See Illustration 10-5.]

PROBLEMS: *Clunk or sharp squeak* (all bikes) A noise heard at each revolution of the pedal, or slight slippage felt, or both. Your *crank is loose* where it attaches to the bottom bracket axle. Don't ride the bike with a loose crank! Especially you cotterless crank people. To check to make sure

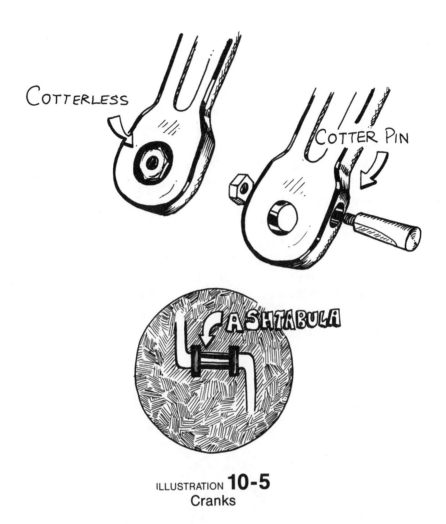

ILLUSTRATION **10-5**
Cranks

that a loose crank is your problem, get off the bike and lean it against a wall, then put the pedals so they are level, one forward and the other back. Get the weight of your body over the pedals. Push down sharply on both pedals at the same time with your hands. Feel anything give? Rotate the cranks 180 degrees and give the pedals another sharp push with your hands. Something give? Watch the joint of each crank and the axle as you push down in order to determine which crank is loose. To fix a loose crank, you need a special tool.

To fix a *loose cotterless crank,* buy a crank extractor and installer; it's inexpensive and easy to use. [See Illustration 10-6.] Some of them are two-piece, like the illustrated tool, but others may be one-piece, requiring the use of a crescent or open-ended wrench. To tighten your loose crank, first unscrew (c-cl) the dust cap (if you have one) with the two-pronged gadget on the installer, or a big screwdriver or the corner of a thin cone wrench if the cap has a slot. If the cap has a 5-mm allen hex key hole in it, you have to use an allen wrench. Some dust caps have tiny little holes; poke the ends of your needlenose pliers in them to get the cap off. When the dust cap is off, take the socket of the installer and put it on the bolt or nut that's in there. Tighten (cl) the bolt or nut, shifting the crank back and forth on the axle as you do, to make sure that it seats properly. Tighten up with a fair amount of torque on the bolt or nut, but don't tighten it so hard that you destroy the threads. If you have new cotterless cranks, repeat the tightening procedure once

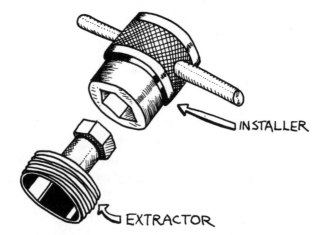

ILLUSTRATION **10-6**
Cotterless Crank Tool

every 50 miles for the first 200 miles of use. If you have cotterless cranks with a nut on a stud, you may have to take the nut off, clean the threads on it and on the stud with degreaser, and put a thread adhesive like Loctite on the threads so the darn thing will stay tight when you tighten (cl) it.

If a cotterless crank won't stay tight, no matter how tight the bolt or nut is, try tightening the crank on the other side to make sure you've been working on the right one. No luck? The crank has a misshapen axle hole.

You have to *replace your cotterless crank.* If you are replacing a right crank, get the chain off the front sprocket and out of the way. First, remove (c-cl) the bolt with the installer. Then back (c-cl) the inner post of the extractor all the way out. Thread (cl) the whole extractor all the way into the dust cap threads. Put the socket of the installer or a socket wrench over the hex head of the extractor post. Screw in (cl) the extractor post until it pushes against the axle, loosening the crank. If the crank won't loosen, tap gently on the end of the extractor with a hammer, then tighten (cl) the extractor a bit, then tap and tighten again. When the crank does come loose, pull it straight off the end of the axle. Extract the extractor (c-cl) from the dust cap threads in the crank. If the threads in the crank get stripped in spite of all your precautions, and the crank is still stuck on the axle, go to a good machine shop and see if they can get it off with a gear puller. Take the old crank, and if possible, the rest of the bike to a bike shop and get an exact replacement. They cost a lot. Don't be shocked.

To install a new cotterless crank, take the dust cap off (c-cl) if it has one. Clean and dry the crank and axle end meticulously, then smear some pipe thread compound, like Never-seez, on the flat surfaces at the end of the axle. Line the crank up so it's opposite the other one (unless you want to try a revolutionary pedaling cadence), and gently slip it onto the axle. Be careful! If you misshape the square hole in the soft metal of your new crank, it will never stay tight, and you will have wasted a lot of money replacing your old one. Get the bolt and washer or the nut, and start (cl) the fastener onto the axle with your fingers. If you have a nut fastener, you might want to clean the threads in it and on the stud with degreaser, then put a thread glue like Loctite on the threads, so the bugger will stay tight. When you have turned the fastener down inside the crank so you can't reach it with your fingers, put on the installer and screw in (cl) the bolt or nut so it's snug. *Don't* tighten it yet. Shift the crank back and forth slightly on the axle when the bolt is snug, then tighten the bolt or nut a bit at a time, making sure the crank is properly seated on the axle. Get the fastener good and tight. Screw in (cl) the dust cap and replace the chain on the sprocket if it's a right crank you replaced. After 50 miles of riding, check the fastener and tighten it again if it can be tightened.

Loose cottered crank (Cruiser) This is a tough one. You might think that all you need to do is to tighten up on the cotter pin nut, but unfortunately, that won't wedge the pin tight enough [see Illustration 10-5]. You can either take a light hammer and tap the head of the pin (the opposite end from the nut), or you can take the bike to a shop where they can use a special tool with an enormous amount of leverage. If you try tapping the pin home, you are endangering your bottom bracket bearings. Any sharp blow on the pin may ram the ball bearings into their races, leaving a row of dents by a process called Brinelling. Brinelled bearings will slow you down and make nasty noises. So, if you can't find a shop with the right tool, you should use some sort of a holder-upper under the crank, so the taps of the hammer will travel down to the ground instead of into the bearings. To make a simple holder-upper, take a 9½-inch piece of ½-inch pipe that's threaded on one end and screw

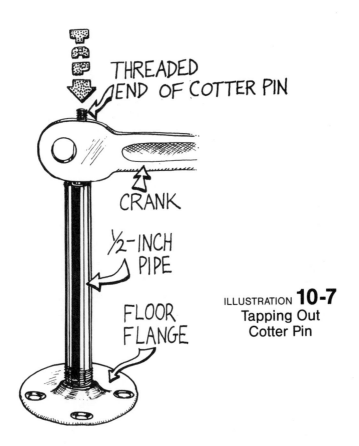

THREADED
END OF COTTER PIN

CRANK

½-INCH
PIPE

FLOOR
FLANGE

ILLUSTRATION **10-7**
Tapping Out
Cotter Pin

a floor flange onto that end. Stick it on the ground under the crank and tip the bike over so its weight is resting on the pipe, as in Illustration 10-7 (but set it up so the threaded end of the cotter is down inside of the pipe, so you can hit the head of the cotter pin). To find out if the pin is seated, tighten (cl) the nut on it, give the head of the pin another light tap, and see if you can tighten up any more on the nut. If you can, the pin isn't seated. Tap more on the cotter pin head. Take your time, make sure you get the pin all the way home. But don't try to do that by tightening the cotter pin nut too tight; they tend to shear off. If you can't get it seated, see the following section.

Cottered crank replacement (Cruiser), though simple, requires caution and a holder-upper. First loosen (c-cl) the little locknut on the cotter until the top of the nut is flush with the end of the cotter. The end should be domed a little, and this dome should just barely stick up above the nut so you can hit it without hurting the nut or the cotter threads. Set the crank on the pipe holder-upper, as in Illustration 10-7. Use a light hammer and make *sure* you tap directly on the end of the cotter each time, so the force of the blow will go straight down the pin and through the crank and the pipe to the ground. When the pin comes loose, unscrew the nut (c-cl) the rest of the way, then take the pin out and take the crank and the pin with you for replacements, which must be *exact*. Put the new cotter pin in so it points down when the other one points up. The pins will *both* point either clockwise or counterclockwise around the axle.

Crank knocking against frame of the bike (all bikes) Your crank is bent; it hits one of the chain stays each time it comes around. (If you have a derailleur gear system and your right crank is hitting the front changer cage, see *Front Changer,* page 209.) Repair requires a special lever that only bike shops have. Don't try to straighten the crank by hitting it with a hammer or prying it with a big crowbar. Take the bike to a reputable shop and face the music, or do the appropriate *replacement* procedure above. Next time, be more careful about which pedal is down as you lean around a corner.

BOTTOM BRACKET

(cl) means clockwise, and usually tightens a bolt or nut.
(c-cl) means counterclockwise, and usually loosens.

DESCRIPTION: (all bikes) The bottom bracket is the part of the bike that holds the cranks in the frame and lets them spin freely. It consists of a heavy axle or spindle (on the Ashtabula set-up, the axle is just the middle portion of the one-piece crank), bearings, a fixed and an adjustable bearing cup, and a lockring for the adjustable bearing cup [see Illustration 10-8]. There are also great sealed-bearing bottom bracket sets made for cotterless crank sets. One note about sealed bearing sets, though: new ones can get a bit loose — just tighten (cl) the threaded ring that holds the whole unit in your bike frame.

PROBLEMS: *Bottom bracket loose or tight* (all bikes) Either your whole axle is loose so that it can slide from side to side, or it is hard to turn the cranks at all. You have to adjust the adjustable bearing cup on the left side of the bottom bracket [see Illustration 10-8].

To adjust the bottom bracket of cottered or cotterless cranks: If you have a shock absorber spanner with a hook on it (see page 20), use it to hook one of those notches in the lockring and loosen (c-cl) it. If necessary, use a light hammer lightly. If you don't have a spanner with one of those nifty hooks, use a screwdriver set in one of the notches of the lockring at an angle, and a light hammer. Make sure you are loosening (c-cl) the lockring. To adjust the adjustable bearing cup, take a small screwdriver and stick a corner of its blade in one of the little holes in the left end of the cup, then tap very lightly or push from an angle to move the cup the way it tightens. You can stick the needle-noses of needle-nose pliers in two of the holes to turn the cup, too. Tighten the cup, then back it off ⅛ turn. Tighten the lockring with the hooked spanner. Cranks still loose? Get a shop to check and tighten the fixed cup if needed.

For a *tight or loose Ashtabula crank* (Cruisers), adjust the left cone. Loosen (cl — that's backwards) the big locknut on the left side of the crank. Put a screwdriver in one of the slots on the left end of the cone (the thing under the locknut). To loosen the cone, turn it clockwise; to tighten the cone, turn it counterclockwise. If the cone is tightened (c-cl) against the bearings and then backed off (cl) ⅛ turn, it will

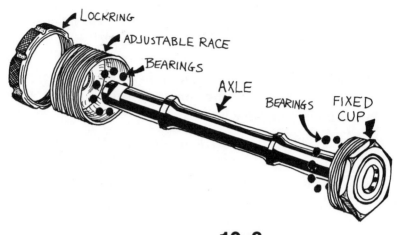

ILLUSTRATION **10-8**
Bottom Bracket, Exploded View

be about right. Tighten up (c-cl) the big locknut when the cranks can turn smoothly without being loose.

If no amount of adjusting will get your bracket right, try a little oil. There are those who think bottom brackets should be oiled regularly. I think oil should be used only as a temporary remedy for bearing complaints. The bottom bracket bearings should be greased well once every year or so, and then left alone. The more oil there is floating around a bottom bracket, the more dirt is going to catch in it and eventually work its way into the works. For greasing, see *Ashtabula overhaul* below.

Nasty noises (all bikes) When you pedal, grinding, or clanking, or grating noises occur that aren't attributable to the pedals. You need to *overhaul your bottom bracket.* Try adjusting it first, just to make sure. If you have cottered or cotterless cranks, see the overhaul procedure just below. If you have Ashtabula one-piece cranks, do the overhaul described on page 170.

For an *overhaul with cottered or cotterless cranks,* (Mt bike, Rd bike) start by getting the cranks off. Remove them as described in **Cranks.** Put the bike upright in a rack or leaning against a wall, over a clean white rag. Get on the left side of the bike. Loosen (c-cl) the lockring on the adjustable cup; stick either a hooked spanner or a screwdriver in one of the notches, and tap lightly with a light hammer. Unscrew the ring all the way and put it in a jar. Start loosening the adjustable cup by sticking needle-nose pliers in the little holes in the end of the cup. When the cup is loose enough that the axle can slip back and forth, reach around to the right side of the bottom bracket and hold the axle tight against the fixed cup on that side. Now undo the adjustable cup with the other hand, working it out slowly, keeping the axle in place against the fixed cup as you go. When the adjustable cup comes free of the frame, pull it straight out over the end of the axle. Collect the bearings — not only the ones that stayed in the adjustable cup, but those nasty ones that stuck to the axle, or fell down inside the fixed cup. Don't turn the bike upside down — the bearings will just run down the frame tubes and hide where you can't get at them. Leave the bike right side up and get all the bearings out with your finger or a little magnet. Count them. Write the number here _____ . Put them all with the adjustable cup in the jar. If the ball bearings are in a retainer ring, you don't have to count them and worry about getting the right number to replace them. Just replace the whole set of re-tainers and balls. What a breeze.

Pull the left end of the axle straight out of the bottom bracket. Catch all the bearings. Count them if they aren't in a retainer ring. Write the number down here _____ . The number should be the same as for the other side. Lock the bearings up in the jar before they run away in search of heater vents or weed patches to hide in.

Look inside the empty bottom bracket shell, or hanger shell as some people call it. Is there a tube of thin plastic that fits around the axle in there? Take it out and save it with the other parts. It is an ingenious device for keeping grit that has gotten into the frame tubes from getting into the bottom bracket bearings and finishing them off. If it's all cracked and ruined, or not there at all, start a shopping list and put that at the top.

Clean out all the grit that has collected in the bottom bracket shell. Clean and look closely at the fixed cup. Use a flashlight if you can't see it well. Is it pitted? Is the shiny ring round, or nearly round? (It sometimes wears a little elliptical from the unbalanced pressure on the cranks, but the shiny place should be very close to round.) Unless the fixed cup is in bad shape, leave it alone. If it is really messed up, you can try to unscrew it (c-cl on most bikes, but *cl* on some English and Swiss and Asian bikes; watch out for that!) for replacement, but go easy, and don't hesitate to take the job to a shop if your tools are inadequate.

When you have all the parts of your bottom bracket (except the fixed bearing cup) in a jar, look at the bearing surfaces on the cups and the axle. Are the shiny rings out of round? Are there any pits or scored places? See Illustration 10-9 if you need to get an idea of what shot bearings look like. Add to the shopping list as needed. Look at the balls themselves. Pitted? Scored? Add to the list, and get extras. Put waterproof bicycle grease on the list. Take the parts you need to replace to the bike shop. Make sure you get the right threads and sizes. Don't use any threaded replacement that is harder to get onto its threads than the old part was to get off. If the threads on the bottom bracket shell are ruined, you have to have the shop cut new threads.

To reconstruct your bottom bracket, lay the bike down on its right side and put grease around the race of the fixed cup. [See Illustration 10-8.] Stick the right number of ball bearings in the grease (if the balls are in a retainer, just stick the whole new retainer in). Wipe off any extra grease. Extra grease attracts destructive grit to the bearings. Find the *long* end of the axle, and stick that end through the fixed cup. If

PITS

SHINY RING

ILLUSTRATION **10-9**
The Pits

you have a plastic tube, slip it into the bottom bracket shell around the axle. Block the frame up a little with a brick or something so the right end of the axle can stick down until the axle rests on the bearings. Hold the axle straight in place and spin it. Smooth? It feels so nice when it is. If it isn't, remove the axle and check for smoothness on all the bearing surfaces. If the axle turns smoothly on the fixed cup bearings, go on to the adjustable cup.

Put grease in the race of the adjustable cup and stick the right number of ball bearings (or the new retainer) in the grease. Put this prepared cup within arm's reach of where you're working on the bottom bracket. Now pick up the frame of the bike, holding the axle in place, and turn it over so the left end of the axle is off the floor. Now reach for that prepared adjustable cup, slide it under the left end of the axle, and screw it all the way up into the bottom bracket shell (cl). Tighten it with your fingers until the bearings seat on the axle. Now you can let go of the right end of the axle. Spin the lockring on; be careful as you start the threads — they are easy to strip. Hand tighten the adjustable cup until it is snug on the bearings, then back the cup off about ⅛ turn, and tighten the lockring, using the hooked spanner or a screwdriver and a light hammer. Tap lightly. Check for looseness or roughness of the axle. If it is just a bit rough, loosen (c-cl) the adjustable cup a bit, and see if you can get a smooth-running axle without getting a loose axle. If you can't, you have no choice but to take the works apart and track down the cause. Check again for grit and scoring on the surfaces. When you get a smooth and snug-fitting axle, tighten up well on the lockring. Go to *Cranks* and reinstall your cranks. Put the chain back on the front sprocket, and you're finished.

(Cruisers) If you have a *one-piece, or Ashtabula crank,* start the *bottom bracket overhaul* by unscrewing (clockwise, remember) the left pedal and taking the chain off the front sprocket. Then get a big wrench, like the Ford monkey wrench or a big crescent if you have one. The channel lock will do if you're careful. Get a good grip on the big locknut that's around the crank on the left side of the bottom bracket, hold the right crank with your other hand, and loosen (clockwise — that's backwards) that big nut. Put the big nut and the washer that should be under it in a jar. Unscrew (cl) the wide left bearing cone. It's the next thing screwed onto the bottom bracket axle. It has two slots in it. Start unscrewing it (cl) with a screwdriver in one of the slots if necessary, then spin it out with your fingers. Hold the crank in place against the right set bearing cone. Don't worry about the ball bearings though. They are in retainers, and they won't jump out and run all over. That's so considerate. Good old Yankee ingenuity. Put the left bearing cone in the jar. Take out the ball bearings, leaving them in their retainer, and put them in the jar. Move the whole axle to the right, tipping it as you go, and ease the whole piece all the way out of the frame through the bottom bracket. Remove all the ball bearings — still in their retainers — from the right side and put them in the jar. Look at all the bearing cups and cones. (The cups are set into the bottom bracket shell, and the right cone is screwed onto the axle.) If any of the bearing surfaces are pitted, or if the balls themselves are scored, or if any of the balls are missing, take the parts to a good bike shop and get exact replacements. If you need to get a cup out of the bottom bracket shell, stick the big screwdriver through the shell from the opposite side and tap around the rim of the cup to drive it out. [See Illustration 5-3 to get the idea.] Using solvent and rags, thoroughly clean and dry the parts you don't replace.

To reconstruct a dismantled Ashtabula bottom bracket set, first screw (cl) the right cone (if you had to take it off) onto the crank. Squeeze bearing grease into the bearing retainers so that all the spaces around the balls are filled with grease. Wipe excess grease off the outside of the retainer rings and set them down on something *very clean* within arm's reach of your bottom bracket. Put one of the bearing retainers onto the crank. Remember that the solid ring side of the retainer goes against the cone. If you put a new cup in the bottom bracket shell, make sure it is well seated. Tap around and around its edges to get it all the way in. Take the right crank in your right hand, and stick the left crank through the bottom bracket without forcing anything. Now put the bearings over the left crank and follow them with the left cone. Remember, the left cone screws on counterclockwise. Tighten the left cone up on the bearings, then back off (cl) about ⅛ turn, or until the crank turns smoothly but doesn't wiggle. Put on the washer, then tighten up the big locknut. Get that nut good and tight, then check to make sure the cranks are still adjusted correctly. Put your left pedal back on (c-cl), get the chain back on the front sprocket, and you're set to go.

CHAIN

(cl) means clockwise, and usually tightens a bolt or nut.
(c-cl) means counterclockwise, and usually loosens.

DESCRIPTION: (all bikes) The dirtiest part of the bike. It has rollers riveted to connecting plates and connects the front and rear sprockets [see Illustrations 10-1 and 10-12]. There are several different standard sizes, none of which are interchangeable. On most cruisers, one link, the master link, has a U-shaped or oversized plate on one side that can be popped on and off. [See Illustration 10-10.] Bikes with derailleurs do not have master links.

PROBLEMS: ***Thrown chain*** (all bikes) Your chain has come off one or more of the sprockets. You need to put it back. Put the chain on the rear sprocket first. Derailleur people: to get your chain back on, first make sure the lever is in the highest gear position, then thread the chain through the tension roller and jockey roller, and over the smallest rear sprocket [see Illustration 10-1].

Everybody, with the back part of the chain the way it's supposed to be, press a couple of chain links down over the teeth at the top of the front sprocket. Crank the pedals forward while holding those links on the sprocket teeth, and the rest of the chain will pop onto the sprocket.

If your chain comes off frequently, it could have any one of the problems described in this chain section. Derailleur people: the most common cause of a thrown chain is a

ILLUSTRATION **10-10**
Master Link

MASTER LINK

changer in need of adjustment — see *Gear Changers: General,* page 191.

Chain sucking (Mt bike) This variation on a thrown chain happens when you are having fun on a mountain bike. That means, you are going fast, getting squirrely, drifting halfway out of control, hammering away at the pedals for all your worth, and loving it. Then, all of a sudden, GRRAACK! The chain gets sucked between the innermost sprocket and the chainstay or a brake arm (if you have brakes mounted under your chainstays).

It's a drag. It sucks, in fact.

A number of things can cause chain suckage, but the most common causes are loose chain flapping around, a bent sprocket, a bent or worn sprocket tooth, or the inappropriate use of gears. First off, don't use the smallest chainwheel when you are riding downhill. It makes the chain loose, and puts it in very close proximity to the chain-suckage danger area, that narrow gap between the small sprocket and the chainstay. Next, check your sprockets for bends or wear (see *Sprocket Problems*). If you have oval chainwheels, you might want to trade them for round ones. Oval ones increase chain flap. If you have a rear brake mechanism mounted under your chainstays, you might consider getting a "shark tooth," a little gizmo you can mount on most brake pivot bolts; it kicks the chain out of that suckage area every time it flaps in there. [See Illustration 10-11.]

Chain jamming, or chain death (Mt bike) The chain falls between two of the chainwheels and gets stuck in there. This is usually due to one of two problems: You are using a narrow chain with chainwheels made for a wider chain, or your chainwheels are not bolted together properly, so there is a gap between them. Get the right chain for your chainwheels, and see *Front Sprocket Problems,* page 181, to fix that bent or poorly attached chainwheel.

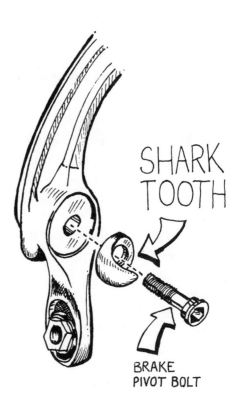

SHARK
TOOTH

BRAKE
PIVOT BOLT

ILLUSTRATION **10-11**

Squeaky or gunk-covered chain (all bikes) You haven't
oiled or cleaned it in a while. It's easy to forget. But it's one
of the few maintenance items that must be kept up with.
Before you oil the chain, see how dirty it is. Depending on
how bad it is, you might take some solvent on a rag and rub
it down, cranking the pedals to move the chain through the
rag, or if it's shot you might even replace it [see ***Chain
replacement*** below]. If the chain is very dirty but not shot,
you can blast the dirt off with water. Spray the chain at a
point between the front and back sprockets, and turn the
cranks to move the chain around so you can spray all of it.
After this treatment, make sure you use a good chain lubricant on the chain. Some people like to use a penetrating oil
like WD-40 first, work it in, wipe it off (a lot of grime will
come with it), then follow up with a good chain lubricant.

Other people prefer to take the chain off as in **Chain replacement,** then soak it in solvent, wipe it clean, and replace it as if it were a new chain.

To oil the chain, get a can of light chain lubricant or motor oil with a thin spout and hold it upside-down over the front of the front sprocket so that the oil will drip down onto the chain as its frontmost point. If you have a multi-speed bike, crank the pedals backwards slowly as you let the oil go from roller to roller of the chain. If you have a 1-speed, foot-brake bike, you can't pedal backwards. Get the bike up on a rack and pedal forwards as you let the oil go from roller to roller of the chain. Go easy on the oil, whichever kind of bike you are working on. It only takes a small drop on each roller all the way around. When you have put that much oil on the chain, take an old rag and squirt a little oil on it. Spread the oil around on the rag, then hold the oily rag around the part of the chain that's stretched between the bottom of the front and rear sprockets. Rotate the cranks back and forth to spread an even, thin film of oil all over the chain. You don't want lots of extra oil on your chain. It attracts grit, which will raise the friction coefficient higher than the oil can lower it. Especially if you ride near the beach where any extra oil picks up stray sand. Go for a ride on your bike with a newly oiled chain. Incredible difference, isn't there? Remember that. Keep the chain covered with a thin coat of light oil. Check it every month in dry weather, every two weeks during rainy seasons.

Loose chain (all bikes) Your chain sags down between the front and rear sprockets. To tighten the chain on cruisers, loosen (c-cl) the big axle nuts that hold the rear wheel to the frame. Pull the rear wheel back in the frame. When the chain is tight enough so you can grab a link halfway between the sprockets and move it up and down only about ½ inch, tighten the right axle nut. Align the wheel so the rim is in the middle of the chainstays, and tighten the left big axle nut (if you need help, see **Wheel Removal** and **Wheel Replacement,** pages 96 and 100).

(Mt bike, Rd bike) The chain is loose on a derailleur system if the rear changer can't take up all the slack chain when the front and rear changers are both in small sprocket positions. Shift both the changers to the large sprocket positions. Is the chain still loose? If, when the chain is on the biggest sprockets, it isn't so tight that it pulls the rear changer forward to an almost horizontal position, you can take a link out of the chain with the chain tool, and connect the ends of the chain back together as described in **Chain worn out.** If removing a link doesn't help tighten up the chain, you probably have a weak or broken pivot bolt spring in your rear changer. [See **Rear Changer,** page 212.] If your chain is as tight as it should be, but still knocks against the chainstay because you do lots of rough terrain riding (as mountain bikers do), you can apply a plastic protector to save the paint on your chainstay.

Tight link (all bikes) When one part of the chain goes over a sprocket, especially a small rear sprocket, the chain kinks. When the same part of the chain comes off the sprocket, it doesn't come completely unkinked. If you suspect that you have a tight link, get the bike up on a rack and crank the pedals slowly. Watch the chain as it goes over the rear sprocket or through the chain rollers [see Illustration 10-1]. Does the chain jump a little each time one link comes around? That's your tight link. You can find the one for sure by flexing the jumpy area of the chain with your fingers until you find the one that doesn't want to flex. When you have found the tight link, mark it.

Before doing anything drastic, try some light penetrating oil like WD-40 on the tight link. Work the oil in by flexing the link with your fingers, not only up and down, but from side to side, so you can loosen up the rivets in the side plates, and make more room between them for the rollers.

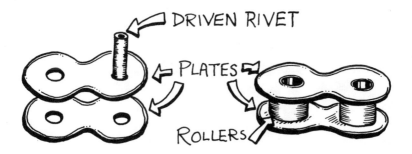

ILLUSTRATION **10-12**
Two Chain Links

No luck? Get your chain tool and turn (c-cl) the handle so the point moves back almost out of sight. Put the rivet of the tight link in the spreader slot (the slot nearest the twisting handle — see Illustration 10-13). Screw (cl) the point of the chain tool until it pushes snug against the end of the rivet. Make sure you have the chain straight in the slot, and the point of the tool butted up against the end of the right rivet. Turn the handle of the chain tool ¼ turn. No more. Back (c-cl) the point of the tool off the rivet and take the chain out of the spreader slot. Is the link looser? Try some oil. Still tight? Try another ¼ turn with the chain tool. Check to make sure the side plates of that link aren't bent. If they are, see *Chain worn out,* below. If the link is no longer tight, look closely at the rivet that you just loosened. Is there more of it sticking out on one end than the other? It's not serious if the difference is very slight, especially on a cruiser bike. On a derailleur bike, both ends of the chain rivet should be exactly equal. On no bike should either end of a rivet be driven in until it is flush with the side plate of the chain. Drive the rivet from the other side of the chain to even things up [see Illustration 10-14]. Test the chain while the bike is still on the rack. Often, a chain that has one tight link will have others that are almost tight. Oil the chain [see *Squeaky chain*].

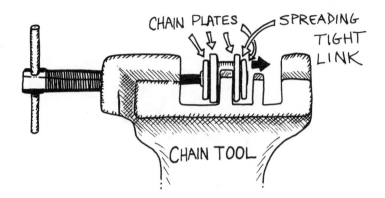

ILLUSTRATION **10-13**
Chain Tool Spreading Tight Link

Chain worn out (all bikes) You're probably hearing lots of kerchunking. Your chain has seen a lot of service, or has been damaged by mistreatment. The chain has a lifespan. You can't expect it to survive more than three years of normal usage, or two years of heavy usage, or a few months of heavy mountain biking. So when your chain starts kerchunking a lot, and you can't find any bad sprocket teeth or tight links to blame the trouble on, test the chain to see if it is ready for retirement. First check the deflection of the chain by moving it from side to side. It should not be so worn that it can deflect more than an inch, even if it is loose on the sprockets.

If there is a lot of side-to-side deflection, grab a link of the chain that is on the front sprocket and pull it forward, as in Illustration 10-15. If the link slacks out as far as the chain in the illustration, then the thing is over the hill. You have to *replace the old chain.*

On cruisers, find a U-shaped or wide plate on one of the links (called the master link). Pry that plate off [see Illustration 10-10]. On derailleur bikes, take the chain tool and put a link in the driving slot (the one farthest from the

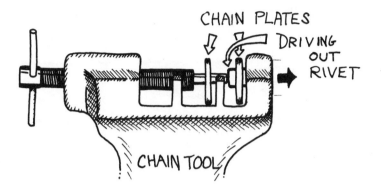

ILLUSTRATION 10-14
Chain Tool Driving Out Rivet

twist handle — see Illustration 10-14). Screw (cl) the driving point in until it hits one of the chain rivets. Make sure the point is butted up square on the end of the rivet. Drive (cl) the rivet out until the end that's *farthest* from the driving point is just flush with the outer edge of the casing of the chain tool, then *stop!* Don't drive the rivet all the way out of the chain [see Illustration 10-12]. Back (c-cl) the point of the chain tool all the way out of the hole in the chain. Take the chain out of the slot in the tool. Does the chain come apart? If not, hold the chain on either side of the driven-out rivet. The rivet is pointing away from you. Now bend both sides of the chain towards you so that the plates spread a bit and release the driven-out rivet. Don't bend the chain hard — you'll just misshape the plates. Take the chain off the bike; go to a good shop and get as high quality an exact replacement as you can afford.

For mountain bikes and road bikes with derailleurs you have to make sure you're getting the same width chain as your old one, then get a longer chain and shorten it to the number of links of your old chain. One end of the new chain will be the narrow link with the roller between the

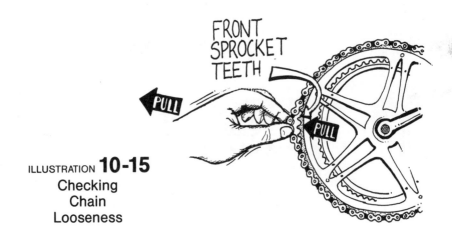

FRONT
SPROCKET
TEETH

PULL

PULL

ILLUSTRATION **10-15**
Checking
Chain
Looseness

ends of the plates. The other end will have two widely spaced plates with no roller between them [see Illustration 10-12]. Remove the extra links of chain from the end with the widely spaced plates with no roller between them. Drive out the rivet of a link that will create a matching end. Put the chain on the bike. Make sure it traces that backwards "S" through the changer rollers, so they pull it tight. Stick the two ends of the chain together, and drive the rivet home (until equal ends stick out the side plates) to complete the new chain. Make sure you have the chain on the bike correctly before you drive in the connecting rivet.

If you have to drive a new rivet to replace your chain, check the link that you have just reriveted. It often gets tightened up in the rivet-driving process. To loosen it, see **Tight link** above. If you replaced your chain because it was old and worn out, you often have to replace the rear sprockets. They wear down too, and a new chain won't fit them. See **Rear Sprocket Problems,** page 186.

(Cruisers) On cruiser bikes, it's a lot easier to put the new chain together if you loosen (c-cl) the rear axle nuts and slip the rear wheel forward a bit. Put the chain around the front and rear sprockets and pinch the master link on with pliers. Pull the wheel back in the drop-outs so the chain is tight, then realign the wheel, and tighten the big nuts.

FRONT SPROCKET (CHAINWHEEL)

(cl) means clockwise, and usually tightens a bolt or nut.
(c-cl) means counterclockwise, and usually loosens.

DESCRIPTION: (all bikes) The round metal wheel(s) with all the points around it that pulls the chain when you pedal. On some cruiser bikes, the front sprocket is permanently attached to the right crank [see Illustration 10-16]. On multi-speed bikes, the crank has three or five arms, onto which one, two, or three chainwheels are bolted. [See Illustration 10-17.]

PROBLEMS: *Kerchunking chain* (all bikes) The chain makes that noise each time it comes to one place on the sprocket. Get the bike up on a rack. Crank the pedals slowly and watch the chain as it goes onto the front sprocket. Does the chain kick up on one of the teeth of the sprocket each time that one tooth comes around? If so, you have a *bent tooth.* If the chain doesn't kick up on any one tooth, continue cranking slowly and watch the chain where it goes onto the rear sprocket, or if you have a derailleur, where it goes through the chain rollers on the changer. Does the chain kick up or jump a little back there every once in a while? Look closely at the chain where it jumps. Is a link of the chain tight? See *Chain Problems,* page 172. Is the chain

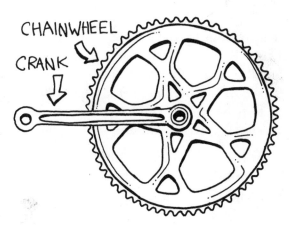

CHAINWHEEL
CRANK

ILLUSTRATION **10-16**
Permanently
Mounted
Crank
and Sprocket
(Chainwheel)

kicking up each time it hits a particular tooth on the rear sprocket? See **Rear Sprocket Problems,** page 186.

(all bikes) If you have a **bent tooth on the front sprocket,** you have to play dentist. Mark the tooth that the chain kicked up on. Take the chain off the front sprocket. On a cruiser if the chain is tight, you have to loosen (c-cl) the rear wheel axle nuts and slip the wheel forward to get the chain loose enough to slip it off the sprocket. [See **Wheel removal,** page 96.] With the chain off the front sprocket, spin the cranks slowly and look down from directly above the front sprocket. Watch closely for the marked tooth and the ones on either side of it. See the way the tooth is bent? If you can't see any bend in the tooth, look at it from the side. If it is chipped or worn down on one corner, you have to replace the sprocket [see **Changing the sprocket** below].

If your close examination of the tooth reveals that it is merely bent, put your crescent wrench on the tooth and tighten it up so that it grips the tooth firmly. Bend the tooth slightly. Take the crescent off and have a look. If the sprocket is steel, you will be amazed at how easily the tooth bends. If the sprocket is Dural alloy, like on the fancy racers' bikes, you will find that it takes a good bit more to straighten a bent tooth. But whichever type of sprocket you have, do your bending in moderation. You want to straighten one tooth, not bend the whole sprocket out of shape. If the whole sprocket gets bent, see below under **wobble.** When you have straightened your bent tooth, put the chain back on. On cruisers, pull the rear wheel back so the chain is nearly tight, then align the wheel between the stays and tighten the axle bolts [see **Wheel Replacement,** page 100]. Try the slow pedaling test. No more kerchunk? Good. If there is still a kerchunk, check the teeth and the chain again.

Wobbly front sprocket (Mt bike, Rd bike) Either one side of the chain or the other rubs against the changer cage at each revolution of the pedal. This is a tough one. Put the

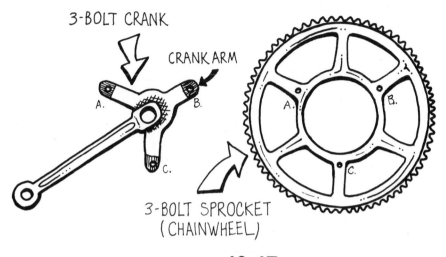

3-BOLT CRANK

CRANK ARM

A.   B.

A.   B.

C.

C.

**3-BOLT SPROCKET
(CHAINWHEEL)**

ILLUSTRATION **10-17**
Bolt-Together Crank and Sprocket (Chainwheel)

bike up on a rack. Crank the pedals slowly, and watch the chain where it goes past the changer cage. Find the area of the sprocket that is bent in or out so that the chain hits the changer cage. Mark the bent area of the sprocket. Sometimes it's hard to tell whether the sprocket is bent in on one side or bent out on the other. Try to decide where the majority of the sprocket is, and call the rest bent in or bent out. Does the bent area that you marked correspond to one of the crank arms? Usually a sprocket with a bad wobble is due to a bent crank arm or a bad connection between the arm and the sprocket [see Illustration 10-17]. Check all the bolts that hold the sprocket tight to the crank arms. They're all tight and you still have a wobble? The only way you can get that thing straight is with a hammer. Take a block of wood and put it against the sprocket where it is bolted to the crank arm (not the crank! — see Illustration 10-17). Give the wood block a good slug with the hammer. *Warning:* That slug can be destructive. The force of the blow will carry through the crank into the bottom bracket bearings and might do some damage there. Brinelling, it is called.

The ball bearings drive right into the surface of their races. They leave a little row of dents so that when you pedal, the bearings have to run over a surface that's about as smooth as a washboard. So, if you are worried about Brinelling your bottom bracket bearings, keep the block in the same place on the chainwheel, but turn the cranks between each slug of your hammer on that block of wood.

Changing the front sprocket on most bikes is easy. Unscrew (c-cl) the bolts that hold the sprocket to the crank, and save all the bolts, nuts, and washers [see Illustration 10-17]. Take the bad sprocket to a reliable bike shop and get a new sprocket that has exactly the same mounting holes. You don't *have* to get one with the same number of teeth, but remember, more teeth will be a higher gear, fewer teeth will be a lower gear. If you change to a larger big sprocket or a smaller little one, you may have to change the length of the chain, and that, in turn, may require a new freewheel and maybe a rear changer with a wider range. All in all, it's easier to keep the new sprockets the same sizes as the old ones. When you bolt on your new sprocket, make sure it's right side out, and tighten up (cl) the bolts a little at a time, working your way around and around the sprocket, so you don't bend the sprocket before you get to use it. Also, make sure all the bolts and nuts are seated as you tighten them.

(Cruisers) If you have a front sprocket that is permanently mounted on the crank [see Illustration 10-16], your crank will probably be cottered, so you will have to do the replacement with a cotter pin tool [see page 162]. If the front sprocket is on an Ashtabula crank, you have to remove the whole crank [see *Bottom Bracket overhaul,* page 166]. Then you can usually spin off (c-cl) the right cone and take off the sprocket. Get an exact replacement, then rebuild the crankset, and you're ready to ride.

Front sprockets misaligned (Mt bike, Rd bike) To test sprocket alignment, put the bike in its lowest gear. Lean it on a wall or put it up on a rack. Kneel down next to the front wheel on the right side of the bike. Put your head way down, just to the front of the front sprockets. Sight straight through the thin space between the front sprockets back towards the rear sprockets. If you see the middle rear sprocket through the thin space, you have a beautifully aligned bike. If one of the other rear sprockets appears in the space between the front sprockets, your power train is not aligned. Aligning is tricky. You might want to have it done by a pro. But if you feel up to doing it yourself, here are some hints.

If you see a sprocket that is bigger than the middle one (a lower gear sprocket), then you have to move the front sprockets to their right, or away from the center of the frame. This can only be done properly by getting a bottom bracket axle with a longer right end. To change the axle, see **Bottom Bracket overhaul,** page 166. If you have Ashtabula cranks, there is no way you can get a longer axle.

If you see a smaller sprocket than the middle one when you sight between the front sprockets, then you have to move the rear sprockets to their right (away from the center of the rear hub). This can be done by removing the rear wheel, removing the freewheel (see the appropriate sections), and putting a thin spacer (washer) between the freewheel and the hub. Shops carry these spacers. This may in turn move the freewheel out on the hub so much that the smallest sprocket hits the bike frame. If so, you have to put a second washer around the rear axle, between the spacer (the long nut with hex sides like a locknut) and the thin locknut. Replace the rear wheel. You may find it hard to fit between the drop-outs. All those washers make a slightly unorthodox rear wheel set-up, to say the least, but the only other alternative is getting a new frame, or having a real frame pro bend your old one.

Back Half: General

DESCRIPTION: The rear half of the power train consists of the rear sprocket or sprockets (which on multi-speed bikes are mounted as a cluster on a freewheel) and the rear gear changer (multi-speed bikes).

REAR SPROCKET (COG)

(cl) means clockwise, and usually tightens a bolt or nut.
(c-cl) means counterclockwise, and usually loosens.

DESCRIPTION: (all bikes) The little metal wheel with the points on it for the chain, which is attached to the right side of the rear wheel. For cruiser people, this part is so obvious and trouble-free that I hardly need mention it. For derailleur people, however, there can be five, six, seven, or eight rear sprockets or cogs, all attached as a cluster to either a freewheel that is screwed onto the hub of the wheel, or a cassette, which is screwed into the hub. The freewheel or cassette has a ratchet inside; that's the reason the bike doesn't go backwards when you pedal backwards; it also lets you coast downhill. The rear sprockets or cogs on the freewheel or cassette vary widely in size, and therefore in number of teeth. The larger a rear sprocket is, the more teeth it has, and the lower it makes the gear. The front sprockets are just the reverse. Say to yourself a few times, "Front larger higher, rear larger lower," to get it memorized.

PROBLEMS: *Kerchunk* (all bikes) Your chain kicks up about twice to every revolution of the pedals. Check first to make sure the kerchunk isn't due to a faulty chain or front sprocket. If a cruiser rear sprocket is causing the kerchunk, remove the wheel [see *Wheel Removal,* page 96], pry off the ring spring that's holding the sprocket [see Illustration 2-14], and replace the sprocket with one the same size. If your derailleur bike has a kerchunk back there, get the bike up on a rack and rotate the pedals slowly. Look closely at the teeth of the sprockets. The gap between each tooth should be a perfectly regular U shape. If the top corners of the teeth are all rounded off, or if one side of the gap between the teeth is worn in at all, then the cog needs replacing. If you have a cassette, you can replace single cogs easily. If you have a freewheel, you need to remove and replace the whole freewheel, or have a shop replace individual cogs.

Cassette cog replacement (Mt bike, Rd bike) Get the bike up on a rack and remove the rear wheel [see **Wheel Removal,** page 96]. Take two chain whips and put them on the innermost (largest) and outermost (smallest) sprockets (cogs) of the cassette, so you can pull clockwise on the innermost cog, and counterclockwise on the outermost cog. [See Illustration 10-18.] The outermost cog will unscrew. When it comes off, remove it and all the cogs and spacers under it and place them carefully in a row on a clean rag. Keep them in the order they came off. This is very important, because the spacers as well as the cogs vary in size and thickness. Get exact replacements for the cog or cogs

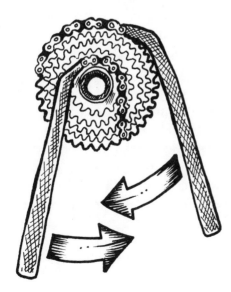

ILLUSTRATION **10-18**
Chain Whips
on Cassette Hub

that were worn or damaged. This is no small feat. Cogs for 5-, 6-, 7-, and 8-gear cassettes of the same brand can be different, and there are custom, easy-shifting cogs of a mind-boggling array of designs. But don't take a poor substitute for your original. They often don't thread on right, or don't work with indexed shifters, or don't work at all. When you have your exact replacement, put it and all the other parts back onto the cassette in the correct order, then screw on the outermost cog, and you're ready to ride.

Freewheel removal and replacement (Mt bike, Rd bike) Note: this procedure does NOT apply to cassettes; if your cassette needs replacement, have a shop do it with their special tools. Get the bike up on a rack and remove the rear wheel [see *Wheel Removal,* page 96]. Unscrew (c-cl) the big axle nut or wing nut or quick-release conical nut off the right end of the axle. (If you have a quick-release, a spring will come off the axle — don't lose it.) Put whichever you have in a jar where you won't lose it. See if your freewheel remover will fit into place on the freewheel around the axle. If it won't, the spacer nut on the axle is in the way. Get a thin spanner and put it on the *left* cone. Get another spanner or a wrench on the spacer nut (the end of the spacer nut is hex-shaped, just like a thin locknut), loosen (c-cl) it, and unscrew it all the way off the axle. Put it in the jar.

Now put the remover in place so that either the splines are well engaged, or the two prongs are set *all* the way down in their slots on the freewheel. [See Illustration 10-19.] Put the big axle nut, or the conical quick-release nut (without its spring) back on the axle and thread (c-cl) it on until it's hand tight. Take a big wrench and get a good grip on the remover. To loosen the freewheel is often very difficult, especially if the wheel and freewheel have been together for a long time or you are a strong rider. Make sure you are turning the remover correctly (c-cl). Also make sure that

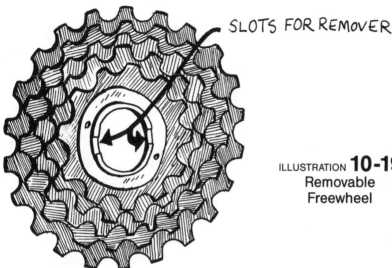

SLOTS FOR REMOVER

ILLUSTRATION **10-19**
Removable
Freewheel

the big axle nut or the quick-release conical nut is holding
the remover snug against the freewheel. Turn the wrench
gradually harder and harder. If you feel something give,
check to make sure the freewheel is coming loose and not
stripping (sometimes, with the pronged remover, the "give"
is from the remover gouging into the freewheel). If the
freewheel comes loose, loosen (cl) the big axle nut or the
quick-release conical nut and spin (c-cl) the freewheel off
the hub. If the freewheel starts to strip, don't try to get it
off — you'll just strip it more. Take off the remover and take
the wheel to a shop. They will hopefully be able to get the
thing off.

When you have spun the freewheel all the way off, you
may find one or two little spacer rings underneath it. Save
these and put them under the new freewheel. You may
have a big wide metal or plastic plate under the freewheel,
too. This is a spoke protector, which is meant to keep the
chain from running into the spokes if your derailleur gets
out of adjustment. If you don't trust yourself and your ability
to keep the gears tuned up, you can keep the protector on
there, but it's a sad sort of statement that you don't even
trust *yourself* to take care of your trusty bike.

Get a good new freewheel to replace your old one if you can. Splurge a little. It makes a difference in the smoothness of the gear operation, and a good freewheel will last longer, too. Whenever you change a freewheel, you usually have to change your chain, especially if the chain is old. Old, stretched chains tend to kick up on new sprockets. You should match the sprockets of the new freewheel with those of the old one. If you want to change to a freewheel with a bigger large rear sprocket, you will have to get more chain. This, in turn, will often tax the tension roller on your changer beyond its capabilities. You will have to change the entire changer system, just to get a slightly lower gear. Changing from a 5- to a 6-, 7-, or 8-sprocket freewheel can also cause all kinds of problems. So can use of a very small (12-tooth) sprocket for the high gear. These work only with a super-strong chain, and even then, they tend to make the chain kick up. They also wear out faster than bigger sprockets. But, if you really think you can go faster with that higher gear, you can go for it.

Put some Never-seez or similar thread compound on the threads òf the new freewheel, then hold the freewheel in one hand, and the wheel (with the spacers on it) in the other, and get ready to start threading the freewheel on. *Careful.* The aluminum alloy used for many hubs is soft. To make sure you get a good start, hold the center section of the freewheel against the axle with a finger and twist counterclockwise, keeping the freewheel exactly vertical, until you feel the threads join. Then twist gently clockwise. Stop immediately if there is any resistance, back the freewheel off (c-cl), using the remover if necessary, and try again. Persevere. When the freewheel finally spins on, it's gratifying. You don't have to tighten up the freewheel. You will do that automatically as you pedal. Put the spacer back on the axle if you had it off, and the big axle nut or the quick-release conical nut and its spring. Put the wheel back in the frame, hook up your new chain [see *chain replacement,* page 178], and you're set to go. After you've ridden the bike a little, tightening the freewheel on well by your pedaling, check the rear changer adjustment, as described on page 198.

Gear Changers: General

DESCRIPTION: (all multigeared bikes) The changers are the devices for shifting gears on a bicycle. The most common gear system is the derailleur-type system in which there is both a rear changer and a front changer. The changers move the chain from sprocket to sprocket, thus increasing or decreasing the gear ratio. This type of system offers a wide range of gears, transmits a very high percentage of your energy to the rear wheel, and is comparatively easy to repair because of its accessibiity. The only drawback is that the derailleur system requires some attention now and then, and you have to use it carefully because of its unprotected location. Don't lay the bike down on its right side, for a start. And don't bump the rear changer or hit it with anything.

The front and rear changers are quite different in design. The front changer is essentially no more than two metal fingers (the sides of the cage) that push the chain from sprocket to sprocket. The rear changer has two rollers through which the chain passes, instead of two metal fingers. The rollers not only guide the chain from sprocket to sprocket — they also take up the slack chain with a spring action when the chain is on a small sprocket. Front and rear changers are discussed more fully in later sections.

Another type of changer shifts cogged planet gears in a hub. This type of changer is most common on 3-speed cruiser bikes. The gears are hidden out of sight and out of harm's way. The planet gear changer, when well built, is definitely the most reliable changer there is. The system requires only oiling and adjustment of the indicator chain. For info on these matters, see the *Hub Changer* section at the end of this chapter. The 3-speed hub has a limited range and the planet gear power transmission is relatively poor. A lot of your energy dissipates in the works of a 3-speed planet gear hub. Also when the hub finally does wear down or when some part of it breaks, repair is an extremely complicated matter — much too complicated to be covered in this book.

Derailleur Systems: General

DESCRIPTION AND DIAGNOSIS: (Mt bike, Rd bike) Derailleur-type changer systems are made up of two control lever units, two cables, and the front and back changer mechanisms.

If you have *gear slippage* of a friction shifter system (a tendency of the chain to slip from a large sprocket to a smaller sprocket, either front or rear) check the *control lever* first (page 201), then the *cable* (page 207), before adjusting the *changer mechanisms* (pages 209 and 212) or doing a *Derailleur System Adjustment* (below.)

If you have an indexed shifter system, and your front or rear changer keeps throwing the chain off the sprockets when you shift into the lowest or highest gear, or if the chain can't make it onto the lowest or highest gear, you need to get the whole gear system aligned and adjusted. On older friction shifter systems, you could adjust the lever, cable, and changer mechanisms, one unit at a time. On indexed shifter systems you have to adjust the whole system at once. See *Derailleur System Adjustment,* below.

Two hints that will save you from many changer problems:

- *Don't ever lay a multi-speed bike down on its right side; and*

- *Don't backpedal a multi-speed as you shift!*

If you have an indexed gear system and the *shifting is rough,* first try a little *Indexed shifter fine-tuning,* as described on page 200. If that doesn't help, do the *Derailleur System Adjustment* procedure below.

If your *chain rubs or makes grindy noises* as you pedal, first fiddle with the lever for the front changer; if that doesn't get rid of the noise, see if the chain is rubbing against the sides of the front changer. If it is, and your lever-fiddling doesn't help, see *rubbing* on page 152. If the grindy noises *still* go on after that, and your chain is oiled, the problem may come from sprockets that are bent or out of alignment [see *sprocket alignment,* page 184]. If all those things check out and you still have grindy noises, maybe you are simply using a combination of sprockets that your bike isn't up to using. On some multi-speed bikes, it isn't possible for the chain to run from the biggest front sprocket to the biggest rear sprocket; on others, it can't run from the littlest front sprocket to the littlest rear one. The chain runs at too sharp an angle; it is either stretched too tight or sagging too loose in these positions. It's a real strain on the system, and it tells you this by grinding and rubbing.

If this is the case with your bike, just avoid using those extreme combinations; the gears can be matched with other combinations. For instance, the gear you get by using the smallest front and back sprockets will be matched, roughly, by using the big sprocket in front and the second to smallest sprocket in back. Surprise! Your bike has two speeds less than you thought.

DERAILLEUR SYSTEM ADJUSTMENT

(cl) means clockwise, and usually tightens a bolt or nut.
(c-cl) means counterclockwise, and usually loosens.

This procedure is for all bikes with derailleurs. It involves putting the bike in its highest gear and adjusting both derailleurs, then putting the bike in its lowest gear and adjusting the derailleurs again.

Adjusting the whole gear system is no small feat. But you can't just twiddle with one part of your system without paying attention to the rest. To get your gears shifting smoothly, you have to adjust all parts of the derailleur system in one procedure. So set aside an hour or so, and go for it.

If you aren't familiar with the parts of your gear system, first look at Illustration 10-20 to get an overview of what's what. Then look at the illustrations of the control levers and the front and rear derailleurs (changers) that are most like yours (Illustrations 10-22 through 10-29). Read the DESCRIPTION sections for the control levers and both changers, too. When you know stuff like where the cable anchor bolts are on your changers, and what the range screws are, *then* start in on this adjustment procedure.

If you have only a rear derailleur on your system, just read and follow the parts of the procedure that cover adjusting the rear changer.

If you have an indexed system, follow the whole procedure, then, if the gears still don't shift real smoothly, do the *Indexed shifter fine tuning* on page 200.

If you have lots of trouble getting an indexed system to work properly, make sure all of the components of the system are compatible. That means that the front and rear changer, the front and rear sprockets, the front and rear control levers, the chain, the cables, and yes, even the cable housings ALL MUST BE OF THE SAME TYPE! In many cases, they have to be of the same model and year of production, as well as of the same brand. This means you should buy a complete system when you install gears, or buy a bike that has a whole system on it. And you have to get replacement parts that match your exact system. There are reasons for this hard-line requirement of gear systems, but I still think it is a crying shame. It may mean that the component pro-

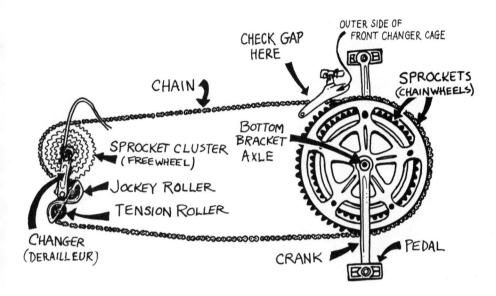

ILLUSTRATION **10-20**
Multi-speed Power Train

ducers can sell a whole lot more parts in the short run, but in the long run, it's such a pain for us consumers that I think it will drive us to to search for more interchangeable parts.

If, as you do the following adjustment, you come across a part of your gear system that has obvious problems, like a cable that's broken or a lever that's loose, just go to the section on that part for its repair.

To start your derailleur system adjustment, get the bike up off the ground, or at least raise the rear wheel off the ground. Put the bike on a shop rack, or up on a floor stand, or hang it on some hooks on your wall or the back of your car, or put it up on your wind trainer. You can have a friend hold the bike up, but the friend may get very tired; the adjustment procedure takes a while, especially if you're doing it for the first time.

If you are adjusting an indexed system, set the control lever to the *friction* mode. There's usually a little mark for friction mode, and a way to twist the round thingie that the lever goes into, so you switch into friction mode. You'll know you're in friction mode when you can move the control lever and not hear any clicks.

Turn the pedals forward and shift the bike into its highest gear. That means the gear where the chain runs on the largest front sprocket (chainwheel) and the smallest rear sprocket (cog). If the chain throws off either sprocket, feed it back on by hand and move the control lever a bit if you have to in order to make it stay there.

If you can get the chain to stay on the largest front and smallest rear sprocket, skip the next paragraph and go ahead with your adjustment.

If the derailleurs are unable to put the chain onto the high gear sprockets, one of the gear cables may be too tight or loose. If the front changer cable is too loose, so you can pull the lever all you want and it won't push the chain onto the big sprocket, push the lever the other way, so the chain goes onto the smallest front sprocket, then loosen (c-cl) the cable anchor bolt on the front changer, tighten up the cable until there is just a smidgen of slack left, then tighten (cl) the anchor bolt and shift that baby back into high gear, so the chain is on the biggest front sprocket. If the rear changer is unable to shift the chain onto the smallest sprocket, first turn the adjusting sleeve [see Illustrations 10-28 and 10-29] all the way in (cl) and back it out (c-cl) about two turns. If that doesn't help, loosen (c-cl) the cable anchor bolt and loosen the cable a bit, so the changer can shift the chain onto that smallest sprocket. Tighten (cl) the cable anchor bolt, leaving NO extra slack. You should have the chain running on the biggest front sprocket and the smallest rear one now. You're ready to get on with the derailleur adjustment. If you can't get into the highest gear even with the cable tension adjusted, then the changers need range adjustment. Read on; that's the next step.

To adjust the derailleurs to the highest gear position, start with the front one and get it aligned and adjusted properly. Look down on the derailleur cage from above. What you should see, when you're in that highest gear position, is the outer side of the changer cage just missing the outer side of the chain, and the section near the cage mount in a plane that's parallel to the biggest front sprocket.

First make sure the cage is lined up parallel to the chainwheel. Look down on the changer and shift it to a lower gear. With the chain off that big sprocket, you should be able to eyeball the plane of the outer side of the changer and the plane of the chainwheel, and see if they are parallel. The outer side of the cage doesn't have to be straight above the chainwheel, but if you can get it straight over the chainwheel, it'll be very easy to see if the planes of both are parallel. If the changer is twisted so the front end of that outer side of the cage either aims toward the bike or away from it, the changer won't work right. Sometimes the leading end of the side of the cage is purposely tweaked in a little, and sometimes there may be a jog in the cage near the trailing end of it, but that's not what concerns you. The central part of the cage, nearest to the mounting thingie that holds it to the rest of the changer, *that's* the part that has to be parallel to the chainwheel. See Illustration 10-26 if you want to be sure you're looking at the critical section of the changer cage. If that section isn't parallel to the chainwheel, shift the changer into the lowest gear (smallest sprocket) and loosen (c-cl) the mounting bolt that holds the whole changer to the bike frame. Twist the whole changer back and forth a bit at a time, until the outer cage is lined up in a parallel plane to the chainwheel. Make sure the changer doesn't slip up or down the frame tube; that outer cage needs to be set so it clears the big chainwheel by about

$\frac{1}{8}$ inch, as well as being in a parallel plane. When the cage is lined up right, and at the right height, tighten (cl) the changer mounting bolt firmly.

Once you have aligned the front changer, put it back in high gear, so the chain is on the biggest chainwheel, and check for a little clearance between the outer side of the chain and the outer side of the changer cage. There should be a gap of about $\frac{1}{16}$ inch. See Illustration 10-20 for where the gap should be. That's about the width of a pencil lead. Not much, in other words. If the gap is too big, or if the outer side of the cage is hitting the chain, tighten (cl) or loosen (c-cl) the high range screw on the front changer. The high range screw is usually the one that's farthest away from the bike frame. Use a small screwdriver to adjust it. The surest way to get it adjusted right is to loosen (c-cl) the screw enough so you can move the changer with the control lever until there's a $\frac{1}{16}$-inch gap between the cage and the chain, then tighten (cl) the high range screw until you see or feel the end of the screw touch the body of the changer. Then back off (c-cl) the screw about $\frac{1}{4}$ turn or less. That should be just right.

Front changer aligned and adjusted in high gear? Good. Now **adjust the rear changer.** Kneel or sit down behind the bike, on the right side, and look forward at the derailleur, which should be feeding the chain up onto the smallest rear sprocket. Find the high range screw; it is usually marked with an "H." If it isn't, you have to peer inside the changer body and figure out which of the two range screws has its tip closest to touching the changer body nub. The tip of the low range screw should be miles away from touching its nub. The tip of the high range screw may even be hidden by the nub it is touching or almost touching. At any rate, when you locate the high range screw, turn it in (cl) until the tip touches the nub on the changer body, then back it off (c-cl) about ½ turn. Now look at the changer from the back of the bike and see if the chain is feeding straight up from the top or jockey roller of the changer onto the smallest rear sprocket. You can take a ruler and line it up with the smallest sprocket, as in Illustration 10-21. If the changer is out too far, or not out far enough, adjust the high range screw until it's right. If the rollers are out of line, so the chain has to bend to go onto the smallest sprocket, then you need to have the changer and/or the back end of your frame aligned. Take your bike to a first-rate shop that has frame-aligning tools and have them do the job. Then adjust the range screw so the chain goes straight up onto the smallest sprocket.

When you have the whole system adjusted so it runs smoothly in the highest gear, switch to the lowest gear. That will mean that the chain is running on the smallest front sprocket and the biggest rear sprocket. If the chain throws off either sprocket, feed it back on by hand and adjust the control lever so it stays on. If the chain can't make it onto one of the sprockets, you may have to loosen (c-cl) one of the range screws a bit, or adjust one of the cables. If the rear changer can't get the chain onto the biggest sprocket back

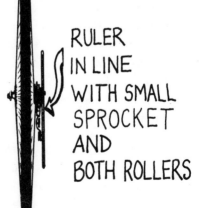

ILLUSTRATION **10-21**
Rear Changer
in High Gear
(Back View)

RULER
IN LINE
WITH SMALL
SPROCKET
AND
BOTH ROLLERS

there, you have to put the changer back in the high gear and tighten the cable. If the front changer won't let the chain go down to the smallest sprocket, you have to loosen the cable to the front changer. In either case, loosen (c-cl) the anchor bolt, adjust the cable length, and retighten (cl) the anchor bolt.

When the chain is running smoothly in the lowest gear, check the low range screws. First adjust the one on the front changer so there is about a $\frac{1}{16}$-inch gap between the inner side of the chain and the inner side plate of the changer cage. Then go back to the back of the bike and adjust the low range screw on the rear changer (it should be marked with an "L") so the chain feeds straight up from the changer rollers onto the biggest sprocket.

Both high and low ends of your gear range adjusted? Good work. Try shifting the gears through the full range. If you have an indexed system, now you can switch the round ring at the lever from friction into index mode. Everything working smoothly? Great!

If an indexed system isn't working just right, you may have to do a little fine-tuning (see below). If you have a friction system, or if fine-tuning doesn't help your indexed system, check the following possible problems: a sticky cable (see *cable replacement,* page 207), a sticky changer (see *changer stickies,* page 214), a loose control lever (see *control lever slippage,* page 203), or damaged sprockets (see *front* or *rear sprocket problems,* page 181 or 186). If the bike has been in a bad wreck, the whole frame may be out of alignment. See a good bike shop for help on this one; tweaked frames can often be saved, if none of the tubes is squished.

Indexed shifter fine-tuning. If you have made sure your indexed gear system is aligned and adjusted as explained above, you still may have to give things a minor tune-up to assure smooth shifting in all gears. Make sure the system is in its indexed mode (set it to *index* at the control lever), then put the front changer in the highest gear, and the rear changer in the second highest gear (for SIS systems) or the highest sprocket (for Sun Tour and other systems). Now turn the adjusting sleeve at the rear changer counterclockwise until you can crank the pedal and just begin to hear the chain pinging against the next lower gear cog. Turn the adjusting sleeve back in (cl) about ¼ turn or so. Try the system in all gears. If it's *still* rough, see the list of possible problems at the end of the derailleur adjustment procedure above.

CONTROL LEVER

(cl) means clockwise, and usually tightens a bolt or nut.
(c-cl) means counterclockwise, and usually loosens.

DESCRIPTION: (Mt bike, Rd bike) There are four basically different types, and both friction and indexed models of each type.

There is a down tube type [see Illustration 10-22], which is usually attached to a boss (mounting bump) on the down tube of the bike frame. All down tube shifters have a long lever that is held in place by a wire wing screw or a screw. They have many little parts arranged around the pivotal screw. On friction system control levers, the wire wing screw can be adjusted while you ride. If your gears slip a little, you just tighten up the wire thing a bit, and continue happily on your way. Indexed systems have even more little parts around the pivot screws. They usually have two settings: one for indexed shifting, and one for friction.

Somewhat similar to the down tube control lever type is the thumb trigger [see Illustration 10-23], which is mounted on the handlebar, a very handy spot indeed. Mountain bikes often use this type. They are mostly for indexed systems, and have settings for indexed and friction shifting, like the down tube levers. Many also have some sort of position

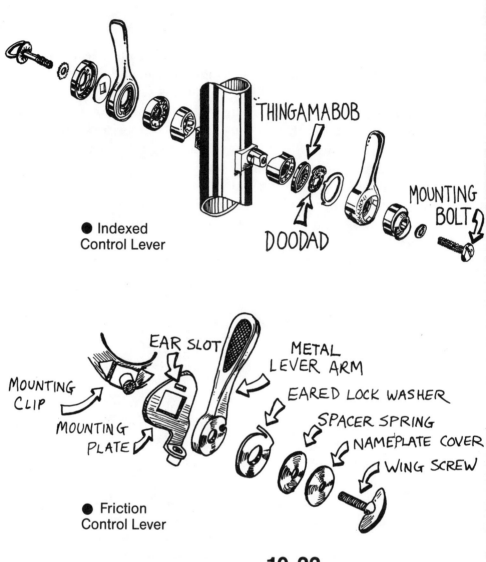

THINGAMABOB

MOUNTING BOLT

● Indexed
Control Lever

DOODAD

EAR SLOT

METAL
LEVER ARM

MOUNTING CLIP

EARED LOCK WASHER

MOUNTING PLATE

SPACER SPRING

NAMEPLATE COVER

WING SCREW

● Friction
Control Lever

ILLUSTRATION **10-22**
Down Tube Control Levers

setting; if you loosen the screw that holds the lever down, you can shift the whole thing clockwise or counterclockwise so you can reach it easily.

An even more convenient position is used for a third type of lever, the double type. The levers are placed under the handlebars on mountain bikes and their city-bred cousins. You press one of the two levers to shift up, and the other to shift down. On some systems, you have to press a lever for each shift (most often when shifting from a low gear to a high gear on the rear changer, or from a high gear to a low gear on the front changer); other systems let you shift through several gears at once.

A fourth type of control lever fits in the end of the handlebar. It is known as a tip shifter. It is held in the bar by an expander bolt that tightens *c-cl* and loosens *cl.* The head of this bolt is hidden under the lever, though, so you have to take the lever off to get at it.

PROBLEMS: ***Slippage or stickies on a friction system lever*** On a friction system, either your lever is very easy to move back and forth, and moves by itself, allowing the gears to shift, or your lever is hard to move, and then moves by itself after you shift. *Don't* oil the control lever. Usually, the problem with a slipping or sticky friction system control lever is the adjustment of the wing bolt or screw. If the lever is slipping,

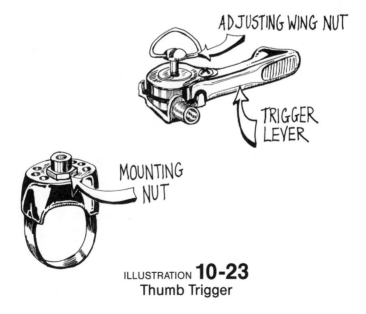

ILLUSTRATION **10-23**
Thumb Trigger

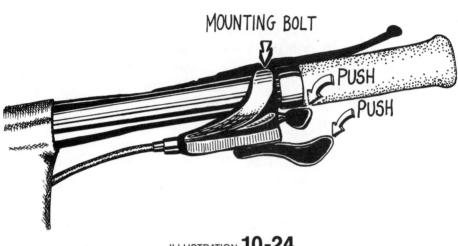

MOUNTING BOLT

PUSH

PUSH

ILLUSTRATION **10-24**
Double Control Lever

tighten (cl) the wing bolt. If the lever is so tight that you
have trouble shifting smoothly, loosen (c-cl) the wing bolt
a bit.

You tip shifter people, loosen the slotted locknut, then
tighten (cl) or loosen (c-cl) the pivot bolt, then retighten (cl)
the locknut [see Illustration 10-25]. If the stickiness persists,
you may have a dirty unit. To clean it, you have to take
it apart by unscrewing (c-cl) the adjustable bolt. Watch it!
There may be quite a few little hard-to-distinguish parts
held together by that bolt. As the bolt comes out, try to
hold things together with your fingers and take them apart
one piece at a time, memorizing the order of things as you
go. The sample I have illustrated is typical, but there are
many variations. Get the order of your parts straight. If parts
spew all over when you take the adjustable bolt off, look at
an identical lever, like the other one on your bike if you
have two. Clean all the rubbing surfaces with a clean dry
rag. Use fine steel wool on the metal parts if you have to. If
any of the parts is badly rusted or bent, take it to a good

shop and get an exact replacement. When reconstructing things, check again to make *sure* they are in the right order. Also, make sure any washer with an ear or "dog" on it (if there is one) goes on so the ear fits in its slot [see Illustration 10-22]. Tighten (cl) or loosen (c-cl) the bolt so that the lever can turn smoothly, but not loosely. Are you still getting slippage? Go on to the *cable* section, below.

Stickies, indexed system levers If you have stickies or rough operation of an indexed system control lever, you usually have to replace the whole lever. Unscrew (c-cl) the mounting bolt that holds the lever to the bike or to the mounting bracket (on many mountain bike levers, the head of this bolt is behind the bracket), take the lever off the bike (see page 31 if you need to take the handlebar grip and brake hand lever off to do this), undo the cable and pull it out, then take the lever to a good shop for an exact replacement. Thread the cable back into the new lever, place the lever (setting it in the comfortable finger position if it's a thumb trigger), then tighten (cl) the mounting bolt. This procedure is relatively simple on most thumb triggers and double lever units, but it can be quite tricky on down tube control levers for indexed systems. The mounting bolt holds a lot of little doodads and specially shaped thingamabobs, often different ones on the left and right levers [see Illustration 10-22]. Agh. If you have to replace a down tube control lever for an indexed system, either have a shop do it, or get the installation instructions for your specific lever, and follow them to a T. If the instructions are written in about six different languages and the English is a little unclear, just take a look at the German version. Whew! They sure use big words, don't they? And with unreal numbers of consonants all in a row. They tell you about things like *Umschalten auf Reibungsschalten.* Oh, yeah. That makes it all clear. Clear that we shouldn't feel too bad about the slightly unclear English version. At any rate, when you are done mounting

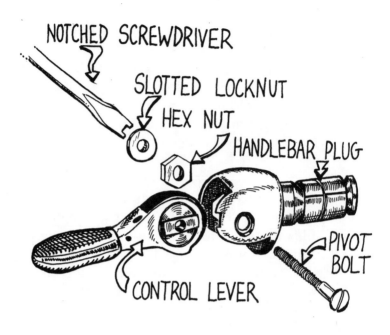

NOTCHED SCREWDRIVER

SLOTTED LOCKNUT

HEX NUT

HANDLEBAR PLUG

PIVOT BOLT

CONTROL LEVER

ILLUSTRATION **10-25**
Tip Shifter

your new gear lever and need to get the cable reset, see the
cable replacement procedure, below.

Broken tip shifter If you have a tip shifter that needs
replacing, take a big old screwdriver and file a notch in the
end, as shown in Illustration 10-25, then loosen (c-cl) and
remove the slotted nut first, then unscrew (c-cl) the pivot
bolt and pull the lever out for replacement. When reassembling, slide the lever in so the square bump fits into the
square slot, then put the hex-nut in its hex-hole and screw
the pivot bolt in (cl) until it is snug. This adjustable pivot
bolt also serves as the tension bolt, like the wing bolt on the
other levers. Tighten it (cl) until the lever works smoothly
but with resistance, then tighten (cl) the slotted nut with the
notched screwdriver.

CABLE

(cl) means clockwise, and usually tightens a bolt or nut.
(c-cl) means counterclockwise, and usually loosens.

DESCRIPTION: (Mt bike, Rd bike) A thin cable (thinner than a brake cable) that runs from a ball, cylinder, or small barrel end in the control lever down to the changer mechanism, where it is held in an anchor bolt. If you have tip or thumb trigger shifters, there will be some housing around the cable, between the lever and a housing stop that is bolted onto the down tube of the frame. All rear changer cables run through a short length of housing that curves down from the chainstay to the mechanism. There are different types of housing for different gear systems. Make sure your cable housing is adequate for your system, especially if it is an indexed gear system.

PROBLEMS: **Stickies** When you shift your control lever, the gears do not change immediately, but wait a while, then shift when you least expect them to. Or they slip just enough that the chain gets hung up between the two sprockets and spins wildly around and around. Put the lever all the way forward. Look closely at the cable where it comes out of the control lever unit, and where it goes into and comes out of any housing. Is the cable frayed anywhere? Replace it if it's frayed at all. Gear cables have to take an amazing amount of strain.

To replace a frayed or broken cable, loosen the anchor bolt on the mechanism and pull the cable out of the housing and the control lever. Get a new cable with the same sort of control lever end.

When you get a new cable, don't cut it to size until you have threaded it through the housing and the cable anchor bolt. When the cable is threaded, push the control lever all the way forward (if you have a thumb trigger or triggers, move the lever to the position that leaves the cable *loosest*). If you are working on a front changer cable, move the mechanism to the lowest gear position. You may have a real oddball front derailleur that won't stay in low, but rather goes to high by itself; if so, just attach the cable with the fershlugginger thing in high gear. If it's a rear changer cable, move the mechanism (or let it spring itself) to the highest gear position. Tighten (cl) the anchor bolt. Try the gears out, and adjust the adjusting sleeve on the control lever or changer if necessary [see *Rear Changer,* page 212].

If your cable is not broken or frayed, but you find grit, rust, and gunk at the housing ends, or a kink in the housing, loosen the cable anchor bolt on the mechanism as if you were going to remove the cable. Pull on the mechanism end of the cable with one hand, and operate the control lever with the other. Try oil on the housing ends. For a rear changer cable, try holding the mechanism end of the cable with one hand and pulling the open section of cable that runs along the chainstay with the other. Is there stickiness in the rear section of the cable housing? If not, test for stickies in the front section of housing if there is one. When you find the area of stickiness, check the housing for kinks, grit clogging it up, or burrs in the ends, and check the cable for evidence of wear. Buy new housing and cable as needed. Get braided housing made for your brand of changer if you have an indexed shifter system. Cut the housing to match the length of the old pieces *exactly.* When cutting coiled housing, work the blades of the wire clipper between the coils, then twist as you cut the wire coil off clean. Check for burrs at the ends of the pieces of housing. Any burr pointing out into the air you can file off. But if there are inner burrs, recut the housing [see Illustration 2-8]. If you have braided housing, you have to snip it off with the diamond-hole kind of cable clippers.

The section of housing where the cable curves under or over the bottom bracket is a common place for grit to gather, especially on mountain bikes. If you have a housing there, and a lot of trouble with grit, you can buy a guide that attaches to the bottom bracket. This set-up will replace the housing, and collect less grit. If the cable binds as it goes through the short piece of housing that passes over the axle of the rear wheel, it may be because this piece of housing is too short or too long. Cut a new piece of housing that can just make the short arch needed to get around the axle without binding on it.

FRONT CHANGER

(cl) means clockwise, and usually tightens a bolt or nut.
(c-cl) means counterclockwise, and usually loosens.

DESCRIPTION: (Mt bike, Rd bike) The front changer has a metal cage that moves the chain from sprocket to sprocket. The cage is attached to a movable parallelogram gadget like the one in Illustration 10-26. A spring usually pushes the side of the parallelogram so the cage goes to the left or into the low gear position. When you pull the gear lever, the cable pulls at the anchor bolt and moves the cage to the right or into the high gear position. A couple of oddball derailleurs are reversed; the spring pushes to the right, the cable pulls the cage left or into low gear.

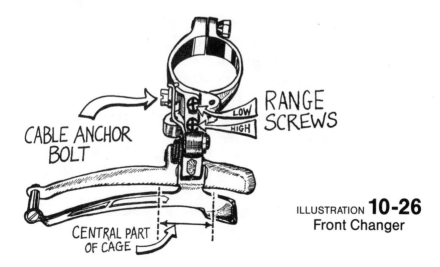

CABLE ANCHOR BOLT

LOW / HIGH RANGE SCREWS

CENTRAL PART OF CAGE

ILLUSTRATION **10-26**
Front Changer

PROBLEMS: *Rubbing* (Rd bike, Mt bike) The cage of the front changer rubs against one side or the other of the chain and makes a bothersome noise. First, try to eliminate the noise with the control lever. Shifting the rear changer often necessitates adjustment of the front changer. Make sure that the adjustable bolt on the control lever is tight enough [see *Control Lever Problems*].

Still got rubbing? Check *alignment* next. Put the bike up on a rack, get your head above the front changer, and crank the pedals slowly, watching the chain where it goes through the cage of the changer. You may notice a wobble in your sprocket. If so, go to *Front Sprocket Problems,* page 181. If the chain hits because it is running at a very sharp angle from the front to rear sprockets, see *sprocket alignment* on page 184.

The next thing to check for is a *misaligned changer.* Are the sides of the cage vertical? If they are bent or bashed out of whack, you should probably replace the changer. If they are in good shape, check to make sure they are parallel with the plane of the front sprockets. If they are cocked in or out, put the changer in low gear, then loosen (c-cl) the bolts that tighten the changer bracket around the seat tube of the bike. Don't take the bolt all the way out — just loosen (c-cl) it a bit. When the bracket is loose, slide it up or down the seat tube until it is at such a level that it holds the changer with the outer side of the cage about ⅛ inch above the large front sprocket. Align the changer so that the *outer* side of the cage is exactly parallel with the front sprockets. Tighten (cl) the bolt that holds the changer to the bike frame and check the alignment from above again. Sometimes the tightening of that bolt will take the changer out of alignment. If it does, loosen it and try again, until the changer is properly aligned.

If the *aligned and straightened cage still rubs,* you have to adjust its lateral position. Find the range screws on the body of the changer [see Illustration 10-26]. Put the bike in its lowest possible gear (small front sprocket, biggest rear sprocket). Figure out which screw controls the inward range of the cage (one of the tips of the screws will be closer to hitting the changer body), and adjust that screw so the innermost side of the cage barely clears the chain. Then put the bike in the highest possible gear, and adjust the other screw so that the outer side of the cage barely clears the chain.

Chain throwing, or changer won't shift chain (Mt bike, Rd bike) When you shift the front changer, the chain falls off the sprocket, or won't shift off it, or gets tangled in the pedals, or catches in the tire and brings you to a grinding halt. Most unpleasant. First check the alignment of the changer and the adjustment of the cage as in **Rubbing,** above, and make sure that when the changers are in highest gear position (big front sprocket, littlest rear sprocket) and lowest gear position, the sides of the front changer cage are *barely* missing the chain. If the cage can move either too far out or too far in, it will throw the chain. If your problem is a chain that always throws off the big sprocket when you try to shift to it, and no amount of adjusting will stop the problem, put your crescent wrench on the front tip of the outer side of the cage, and bend it in very slightly, about $\frac{1}{16}$ inch. This slightly bent-in cage tip will catch a chain that has throwing tendencies.

If your adjusted front changer can't get the chain *onto* one of the sprockets, the cable may be either too tight or too loose. Loosen (c-cl) the anchor bolt that holds the end of it and tighten or loosen the cable, as needed. Then tighten (cl) the anchor bolt and check to make sure the changer is still adjusted right.

If your chain throws off one of the front sprockets all the time, not just when you are shifting, you might have a very old, flobby chain. See **Chain Problems,** page 172. If the chain is in good shape, the problem is the alignment of the front and rear sprockets. See *sprocket alignment,* page 184, in the Front Sprocket section.

REAR CHANGER

(cl) means clockwise, and usually tightens a bolt or nut.
(c-cl) means counterclockwise, and usually loosens.

DESCRIPTION: The thing that changes the chain from one rear sprocket to the other. It consists of a changer body and a cage with two chain rollers, one of which holds the chain tight (the tension roller) and one of which moves the chain from sprocket to sprocket (the jockey roller). There are two distinct types of rear changers. One has a box-like body with two closed sides [see Illustration 10-27]. The range screws may be in different places, and the cable anchor bolt may be easier or harder to get at, but the design is usually very similar. The other type is the slant pantograph, shown

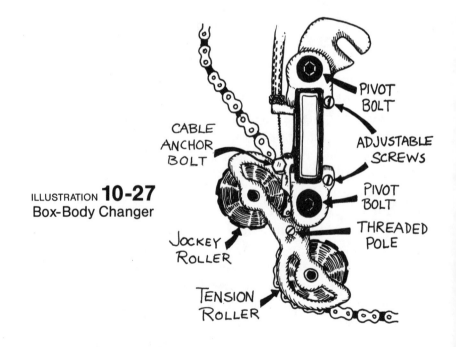

ILLUSTRATION **10-27**
Box-Body Changer

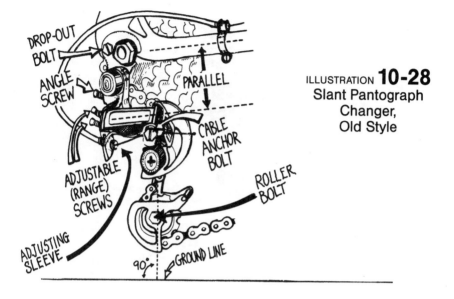

ILLUSTRATION **10-28**
Slant Pantograph
Changer,
Old Style

in Illustrations 10-28 and 10-29. They work great if you set them at the right angle. To do this, put the changer into the highest gear and adjust the angle screw so the changer body is parallel with the chainstay of the bike. While the changer is still in the highest gear, check the roller cage and see if it is pointing straight down at the ground, as shown. If it isn't, lengthen or shorten the chain until it is. The range screws are used as the ones on a solid body changer, and are usually marked with "H" and "L" for high and low; a nice touch.

PROBLEMS: *Chain throwing or not making it* The changer throws the chain off, or won't put the chain onto the biggest or smallest rear sprockets. Your changer needs to have its *alignment* and *adjustment* checked. See the *Derailleur System Adjustment* procedure, page 193. If you find that your rear changer is out of alignment, take the bike to a first-rate shop with frame-aligning tools, especially if you have an indexed gear system.

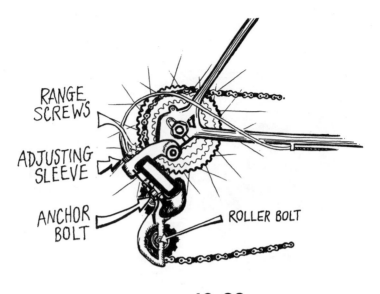

RANGE SCREWS

ADJUSTING SLEEVE

ANCHOR BOLT

ROLLER BOLT

ILLUSTRATION 10-29
Slant Pantograph Changer, New Style

Stickies The changer is sluggish in shifting from one sprocket to another, especially onto the smallest sprocket, and you have checked the control lever and the cable. Try a little oil first, at the joints of the changer body where it flexes when you change gears.

If oil and a good workout don't help the stickies, your only recourse is to replace the sticky changer. See the *Changer replacement* section below.

Chain loose, or feeding roughly Either your chain sags when the rear changer is in the high gear positions, or your changer does not shift smoothly, and grindy chain noises often appear. First check the chain [see *Chain Problems,* page 172]. Next, take a good look at the changer, especially the chain rollers and their cage. Are the rollers covered with gunk? Is the pivot of the cage all gunked up? You may need to clean the rollers and the cage. Take them apart slowly and carefully, making sure you memorize the order of the little sleeves and washers around the pivot bolts. Oil each roller with the lubricant you use on your chain, and reassemble it, leaving plenty of play for the ball bearings if you have them. If the rollers are always getting dirty and sticky, you can get a pair of rollers made with sealed bearings, by Bullseye. They're available from catalogues, and although they cost a pile, they last forever, so they're worth it.

If the cage and rollers are not only dirty but bent out of shape, so the chain runs cockeyed, don't try to bend it back straight again; you'll just get it all sticky in its joints. See *Changer replacement,* below.

If there is a spring that you can see hooked onto the roller cage, is it broken? If so, replace it. If the part of the changer that holds the spring is banged up, replace the whole changer.

Has the spring come loose or unhooked? Reset it carefully with pliers. Don't let it nip you in the process. If you can't see any tension spring on your changer, it's probably inside a cylinder around the lower pivot bolt, the bolt that holds the roller cage.

To tighten this hidden spring, you have to loosen whatever's holding it in place, then tighten the spring, then tighten the holder. Start by removing any cap that is on the end of the pivot bolt. When the cap is off, you'll see either a "castellated" bolt end under there or a simple hex-shaped hole for an allen wrench.

If there's a castellated bolt (one that looks like the turret of a castle), you just take off (c-cl) the little threaded pole on the cage, spin the cage (cl) until it is loose, then move the hook end of the spring from one slot in that turret thing to the next slot in a counterclockwise direction. Now wind the spring back up, put the threaded pole back in (cl) and screw the cap back in (cl) to hold the whole works together.

If you have a hex hole in the end of your pivot bolt, put an allen wrench in it and hold it still, then undo (c-cl) the nut or the cage itself at the other end of the pivot bolt. You may need to undo (c-cl) a threaded pole if you want to turn the whole cage around, and you may have to take off the tension roller and remove the chain for the same purpose.

Keep holding that pivot bolt for a moment, so the spring doesn't go loose, then figure out how you can tighten the spring. It can be done in lots of different ways, depending on the changer. If there is a locknut right next to the cage, loosen the cage and the locknut (c-cl), then turn the pivot bolt (c-cl) so the spring tightens, then tighten the locknut against the cage (cl). On other changers you have to take the cage off and turn it clockwise so the end of the spring can fit into a different little hole which will bring up the tension when the whole thing is put back together. On some models, the only thing you can do is turn the whole cage once counterclockwise and then put the threaded pole back in. This will make the spring really tight, so be careful. Tighten up the cage or nut on the pivot bolt when the spring is tight, no matter which set-up you have.

Changer replacement is a good alternative to overhaul and alignment, if you can afford it. Any bent changer, or changer with corners and edges knocked off, should be replaced. Start by removing the rear wheel. Then loosen (c-cl) the cable anchor bolt and remove the cable. Unscrew (c-cl) the bolt that holds the changer to the frame drop-out, and take the changer off. Undo (c-cl) one of the roller bolts and remove the roller to release the chain from the roller cage. Take the changer to a good shop and get a new one. Get one that's exactly like your old one, especially if you have an indexed gear system. You may have to get the latest version of your model — let a good bike shop help you in this case. Tighten the mounting bolt of your new changer into the drop-out, being careful not to mash the tip of the angle screw against the drop-out tab. If the mounting bolt has a nut that goes on the back of the drop-out, spin the nut on, loosen (c-cl) the mounting pivot bolt about ¼ turn, then hold it still with the allen wrench while you tighten (cl) the nut back behind the plate. Take the tension roller (the lower one) out, loop the chain over it, and replace it so that the chain makes a reverse "S" through the rollers. Tighten (cl) the roller bolt up again. If the roller has ball bearings (rare), check to make sure that the roller turns freely without being so loose that it wobbles. Adjust the two cones (cl is tighter, c-cl is looser) as needed (for more info on ball bearings, see *Hubs,* page 103). Connect the cable to the cable anchor bolt, and adjust the range-limiting screws so that the changer shifts smoothly into the largest and smallest sprockets without throwing the chain [see *Derailleur Adjustment,* page 193].

Hub Changers

(cl) means clockwise, and usually tightens a bolt or nut.
(c-cl) means counterclockwise, and usually loosens.

DESCRIPTION: (3-speed cruiser) This system consists of a control lever, which is usually mounted on the handlebars, a cable that is partially housed, an indicator chain, which is adjustable, and a mechanism in the hub of the rear wheel. When problems occur, always remember that they might be due to trouble in any or all of the three units — control lever, cable, or mechanism.

PROBLEMS: *Gear slippage or loss* (3-speed cruiser) Your middle gear, the one with the "N" on the control lever, suddenly changes from "N" for Normal to "N" for Neutral. Your feet fall off the pedals, and you make a painful landing on the top tube of the bike, or if it's a women's bike, the down tube. Ouch. You may discover your slippage in a less painful way. Often the control lever can't get the hub into the low or middle gear at all.

The cause of gear slippage, in 99 cases out of 100, is improper lubrication and adjustment. (In the 100th case, when slippage cannot be corrected by oiling and adjusting,

take the wheel out as in **Wheel Removal,** page 96, and take it
to a good shop for overhaul.)

To oil the 3-speed hub, find the lubricating nipple on
the hub casing and squirt in about three healthy slugs of
fine, light oil like Sturmey Archer or Automatic Transmission Fluid (the pink stuff). Put a drop or two in the control
lever, too.

To adjust the hub, put the bike up on a rack and put it in
high gear. Make sure that the hub, not just the control lever,
is in high gear. Loosen (cl) the knurled locknut on the
indicator. Tighten (cl) the sleeve by hand until there is only
a little slack in the cable. Lock (c-cl) the locknut up against
the sleeve. Next, get the control lever into the "N" or middle
gear. Look closely at the indicator through the hole on the
side of the long pole-shaped nut that the indicator goes
through. In that hole, you should be able to see the end of
the axle. If the indicator is in the middle gear position, the
shoulder of the smooth pole that goes into the middle of
the hub [see Illustration 10-30] should be just visible, sticking out of the end of the axle. Adjust the sleeve on the

indicator if necessary. Tighten (c-cl) the locknut. Still getting slippage? Make sure the metal band that holds the cable fulcrum ferrule is cinched tight around the frame. If it slips, the gears slip. If it's solid, maybe the indicator is messed up, or not screwed in all the way. Shift the lever to the high gear. Remove (c-cl) the sleeve from the indicator completely. Try screwing (cl) the indicator into the hub farther. Don't get rough with it — it's delicate. Just tighten it by hand. But try to get it screwed in until it's snug. If you have to back it off (c-cl) a half turn or less to get the chain going at an angle that allows flex, that's OK, but don't loosen it any more than that. If the indicator is rusty or all mashed and bent, take it

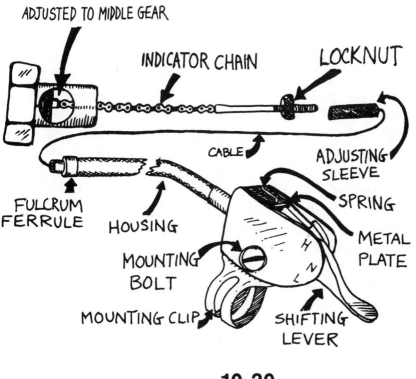

ILLUSTRATION **10-30**
3-Speed Gears

out (c-cl) and go to a bike shop for a new one that's the same size. Get a spare while you're at it. Put in (cl) the new indicator, making sure that you get it all the way in until it is snug. Put the sleeve on and tighten (cl) it until there is only a little slack in high gear. Tighten up (c-cl) the locknut. Shift the lever to the middle gear and check the adjustment at the end of the axle. Get it right. Make sure you tighten (c-cl) the locknut well (but without using any tools that will mash it) when you are finished. Ride in peace. You won't be hitting that top tube for a while.

Cable broken (3-speed cruiser) First look at the whole cable and control lever set-up. Is everything pretty old and grungy? Is the lever messed up so that it slips all the time? Consider getting a new handlebar control lever [see Illustration 10-30], especially if your messed-up one is one of those in the hand grip, or one of those plastic monsters on the top tube. Get a standard handlebar-mounted hand lever. They're more reliable.

To get an old cable off a bike, you have to remove the big clamp that holds the fulcrum ferrule to the frame of the bike. Loosen (c-cl) the screw that holds on the clamp. Get the end of the housing, and the ferrule (the little plastic or metal sleeve) that holds it, out of the clamp. If you are sure your control lever is OK, get the end of the cable out of it.

For ball bearing lever (or hand grip) people, unscrew (c-cl) the screws that hold the casing of the control lever together, and catch the ball bearing and its little washer as they fall out. Take the end of the cable out of its slot. Look at the race that the little bearing was running in from pocket to pocket for the different gears. If that race is worn into the metal, replace the whole lever.

To get the cable out of a standard lever, pry up the little flat piece of metal with a wire spring on it that is at the top of the control lever [see Illustration 10-30]. Push the cable from the outside of the control lever, so the end comes up

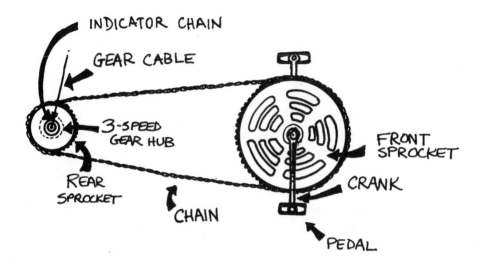

ILLUSTRATION **10-31**
3-Speed Power Train

out of its slot, then pull the cable end back under the little flat piece that you pried up and out of the control lever.

Take the pieces of the old broken cable and the housing to a bike shop. Get a new cable and housing that are the same length as your old one, and get a new control lever if you can find any excuse to; they can save you from so much pain. Get a new ferrule for the end of the housing if your old one was beat up or decayed with age. Put the ferrule around the end of your new housing and push the indicator sleeve through the hole in the clamp that holds the ferrule. Then push the ferrule into the clamp. To put the end of the cable in the new control lever, pry up the little piece of metal with the spring over it in the control lever [see Illustration 10-30], and push the end of the cable through until it sticks out from under the little flat piece. Put the control into the high gear position and slip the end of the cable down into its slot.

Thread the other end of the cable over its roller, and screw (cl) the sleeve onto the indicator. If the cable is too long or too short, you can adjust it to roughly the right length by moving the big clamp that holds the housing end ferrule up and down the frame. When you get them right, make sure the ferrule is holding the end of the housing so that it is seated. If no amount of adjusting the clamp will get your cable short enough, you can try to get another cable that's shorter, or you can get a cable with an adjustable sleeve. It has a little cable anchor bolt on it that you can tighten up anywhere on the cable. Just make sure you get it *tight* on the cable, so there's no chance of it slipping a bit and causing you to hit that top tube when the gears go into neutral. Adjust the cable as in the procedure in **Slippage,** above.

Appendix

Anything on bicycle that isn't absolutely essential to its function is vestigial. Extra. Dead weight.

Some extras, which I will list first, can be worth their weight. The others make me feel like I have appendicitis if I write about them, so I refuse to say much at all.

Toe clips. The little metal or nylon frames with straps that attach to the pedals and hold your feet in place. If you don't have clipless pedals, these are a must for long-distance riding. Like clipless pedals, they make it easier for a rider to keep an even pace, and they save all the energy you would waste trying to keep your feet in place on the pedals. There are different sizes. Get ones to fit you, and make sure they are bolted on well.

Mud guards (fenders). A useful vestige when it's raining. Make sure they are bolted well at all brace ends. If the braces rub the wheel, loosen (c-cl) the bolts that hold them to the frame and adjust, then retighten (cl) the bolts. That's better than bending the braces out like wishbones. For extra water protection, glue or tape pie-shaped pieces of plastic sheathing from the drop-outs to the mud guard between the braces. These pieces are most needed at the back of the front wheel and the front of the back wheel. Don't expect them to keep you completely dry, though. Riding in the rain is a pain. To reduce the pain in cold weather, put plastic sandwich bags over your socks before you put your shoes on, and wear waterproof gloves.

Helmet. A must for any serious cycling, especially in traffic. There are many high-quality hard shell and soft shell cycling helmets. If you shop around, you can find one that's

HELMET HISTORY

comfortable, light, cool, and up to the safety standards. It may cost a bundle, but you should consider it money well spent; heads are one to a customer.

Carrier. For cycle tourists, the Blackburn carriers are unbeatable. They cost, and getting one to fit your bike can be a pain, but they last, which is critical on a long tour. For light-duty use, though, you can get cheaper ones that don't have to be custom-fit to your bike. The carrier goes behind the seat, over the rear wheel. Make sure all bolts and nuts for it are kept tight. You can use self-locking "aircraft" or "nylock" nuts; they don't shake loose. You can also get all kinds of other fancy racks and bags and panniers for your bike. I don't like having stuff like that on a road or mountain bike. I have a cruiser with a big basket for shopping. When I'm riding for fun on a lightweight bike, I just take a banana or two and my windbreaker in my jersey pockets. If I have to carry a little something extra, I use a little cloth rucksack, which I fold up and put into my pocket after I've eaten the little something. That rules out camping on a bike for me.

Pump. For road bike people, a good, solid frame pump is a must. Mountain bikers who do long treks, or who like to change the amount of air in their tires during a ride, should get a super-solid model. But casual mountain bikers and

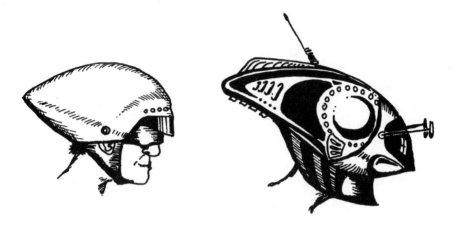

short-ride cruisers rarely need a pump en route. If all you do are short rides on wide, thick-treaded tires, get a good floor pump for your garage, or use the gas station air carefully, making sure not to over-inflate.

Water bottle. The plastic kind that fits in a little wire cage that's clamped to the frame. Only needed on long, dry rides. On *very* long, dry rides, you may need two or even three bottles. Get one made out of tasteless food-grade plastic. You can put stuff in the water to replace the electrolytes and salts you lose as you sweat. Just make sure you don't OD on the commercial stuff. I find a little V8, a bit of fruit juice, and a lot of water do the trick.

Kickstand. These are useful on cruisers. Make sure the bolt (if there is one) that holds the stand tight between the chain-stays is *extra* tight. If your stand is a little too long for your bike (the bike stands up too straight and falls over easily), try leaning the bike on the stand, then picking up the rear wheel 3 inches so the weight of the bike is on the stand. Now push down from straight above the stand so that it bends until the rear wheel comes back to earth. Bike leaning over more? It should be. If your crank hits the kickstand, loosen (c-cl) the bolt that holds the stand, move the stand, and tighten (cl) the bolt well.

Light. There are cheap simple ones with batteries, expensive bright ones with batteries, and really high-tech generator ones. The cheap little arm-band light works OK for making you visible to motorists. The similar blinking model is brigher, yet lasts longer. You can clip the blinker type to your shoe. Strap the arm-band light to your leg, not your arm; put it just below the knee so it bobs up and down when you pedal. It might save your life. You can use one of these in combo with a bright battery-powered headlight, and get along pretty well in the dark, as long as you only need to make a short trip. Most other lights with generators, remote rechargeable batteries, wires, directional signals, toggle switches, and other such vestigial crap are not only unaesthetic — they can be dangerous because they can get caught in the works of your bike, and they often don't work after rough usage on the road. If you find long night rides without a headlight spooky, stick to daytime riding. Simple enough?

Lock. The best lock is the human eye. If you have a good bike, take it inside with you, or lock both wheels with a U-type lock to something outside a window that you can keep glancing through. Keep your eye on it. Don't leave a good bike locked with any lock outside overnight. Oh, jeez, I get bad vibes talking about locks. I'll never get over having my dear old Cinelli ripped off. Put it this way. If you steal bikes, for God's sake, stop it. If you steal a bike from someone who loves it and depends on it, you are doing one of the lowest things that one human being can do to another. Steal something else if you have to steal.

Chain guards. Hard to keep from hitting on them with the crank and other things, isn't it? I agree. If yours is troublesome, take it off, and put a rubber band or a pants clip around your cuff.

Brake-lever extensions, polycarbonate designer goggles, gold-plated corkscrews, "chopper" forks, "sissy" bars, chromed tailpipes, imitation leopard skin saddle covers. Filth, filth. Filth and junk. I refuse to say more about them.

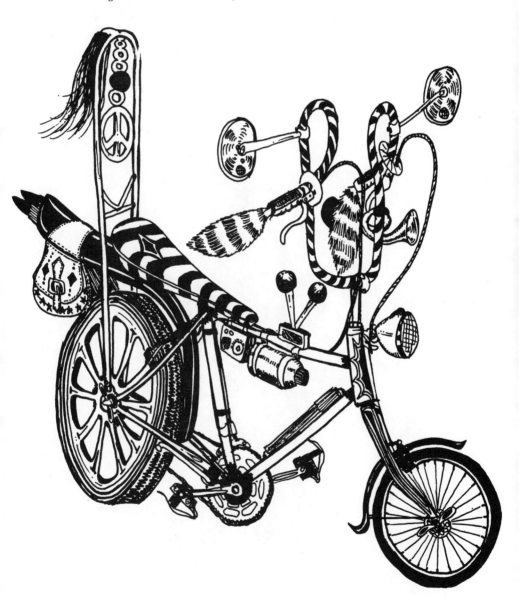

Postscript

This isn't the end. Tomorrow I'll probably find some problem I haven't covered in this book. Or, more likely, *you* will find something I didn't cover well enough. If you do, write to me about it so I can make this book better in the future. I hope there will always be two more bicycle problems — one that I can tinker with, and one that you can tinker with.

Write: Tom Cuthbertson, c/o the publisher.

Index

E

Einstein, 6
Eisentraut, Al, 140
Expander bolt, in stem, 75
Extension (stem), length of, 77

F

Fenders (mud guards), 223
Ferrule (shim), for handlebar stem,
    69-70, 79
Ferrule (sleeve)
  on brake cable, 35
  on gear cable, 219
Fifteen-speed bike, 4. *See also*
    Mountain bikes
File, 25
Five-speed bike, 4
Flat tires, 126-35
  preventing, 133, 134-35
Floor stand, 26
Foot brake. *See* Coaster brake(s)
Fork, 91-93
  bent, 94
  headset and, 81
Fork crown race, 81, 83. *See also*
    Headset
Frame, 137-40
  bent, 140
  in buying decision, 9
  painting, 140-41
Frayed cable, replacing, 207-9
Freewheel, 186
  replacing, 188-91
Freewheel remover, 25
  using, 188-89
Friction shifting system
  See also Derailleur system
  adjusting changers in, 195-200
  control levers on, 201-3
  slippage or stickies in, 203-5
Front changer, 191, 209
  adjusting, 196-98, 210-11
  aligning, 210
  chain throwing on, 211-12
  rubbing, 210-11
  won't shift, 211-12
Front half (power train), 149-50,
    151-53. *See also specific parts*
Front sprocket (chainwheel), 181
  bent tooth on, 181-82
  changing, 184-85
  misaligned, 184-85
  wobbly, 182-84
Front wheel
  removing, 96-97, 99
  replacing, 100-101, 102

G

Gear cables, 207-9
  broken, 220-22
  grit, rust, or gunk on, 208-9
  housing for, 207, 208-9
  removing, 220-21
  replacing, 207-9
  stickies in, 207
Gear changer, 191-92
  See also Derailleur system; Friction
    shifting system; Hub
    changer; Indexed shifting
    system
  checking, 15, 16
  control levers, 201-6
  diagnosing problems in, 150-51
  noises from, 150
  rubbing on chain, 152
Gears, slipping, 152, 192
Getting a bike. *See* Buying a bike
Gooseneck. *See* Stem
Grating noise in bottom bracket, 166
Greasing bearings, 16. *See also specific
    parts*
Grinding noises
  in bottom bracket, 153, 166
  in derailleur, 193
  in headset, 84
Grips. *See* Handlegrips

H

Hammer, 19
Handlebars, 67-69
  drop bar bent in, 70-71
  loose in stem, 69-70
  replacing, 71
  stem height and, 77
  tape worn or unwound on, 71-73
  too high or too low, 70
Handlegrips, removing, 71
Hand lever unit (brakes), 31
  slippage in, 33-34
  stickies in, 31-32
Headset, 81-82
  checking bearings in, 15-16
  cracking or grinding in, 84
  loose, 82-84
  overhauling, 85-90
  stiff or sticky, 84-85
Head tube, 137
Height of handlebars, 70
Height of seat, 146
Helmet, 223-24
Hex-setscrew (Allen) wrenches, 21-22

 *Other Ten Speed Press books you may enjoy:*

BIKE TRIPPING
by Tom Cuthbertson   Illustrated by Rick Morrall

The other classic in the field. This revised edition covers everything you need to know to have good trips on a bike. Individual chapters discuss commuting, short joy rides, day tripping, and serious touring. $7.95 paper, 272 pages

THE BIKE BAG BOOK
by Tom Cuthbertson   Illustrated by Rick Morrall

". . . belongs in the backpacks of any backroad bicycler."
—San Francisco Examiner-Chronicle

No matter how light you travel, you should have enough room for this little book, which distills emergency road repair tips from ANYBODY'S BIKE BOOK. Covers what tools to bring, trouble-shooting, and temporary repairs on the go.
$3.95 paper, 144 pages

THE URBAN ADVENTURE HANDBOOK
by Alan North

Adventure does not only happen in the wilderness! With tongue in cheek, this book introduces the idea of heart-pumping, adrenaline rush escapades to be had in the city. Definitely not sports in the usual sense, and not recommended for the faint of heart, these adventures involve biking, climbing, and exploring at the edge of sanity. Illustrated with photos and line drawings. $11.95 paper, 160 pages

AUTO REPAIR FOR DUMMIES
by Deanna Sclar

A book for anyone who is terrified of fixing their car—or of mechanics! Concise, direct, simple explanations help the reader understand any car's major systems, and take the fear out of dealing with maintenance and repair. Special sections cover buying a new or used car, finding a good mechanic, and keeping your car looking good. Over 300 illustrations and photographs. $17.95 spiral or $26.95 clothbound, 480 pages